THE AGE OF THE ECONOMIS

83

HB-
F/1

HF
75
.F87
196

DANIEL R. FUSFELD   ●   University of Michig

SCOTT, FORESMAN AND COMPA

Introduction

Edmund Burke called the eighteenth century "the age of the economist," and the label is equally appropriate for our own time. The writings of economists have defined the major social philosophies of the past two hundred years. The chief ideological debates of the modern era have involved the basic ideas of great economists like Adam Smith, Karl Marx, and John Maynard Keynes, who achieved their stature primarily because of the social philosophies involved in their economic theories rather than because of the scientific advances they made.

This fact was well understood by Keynes himself, who, doing battle with ideas he was convinced were wrong and pernicious, wrote:

> The ideas of economists and political philosophers, both when they are right and when they are wrong, are more powerful than is commonly understood. Indeed the world is ruled by little else. Practical men, who believe themselves to be quite exempt from any intellectual influences, are usually the slaves of some defunct economist. Madmen in authority, who hear voices in the air, are distilling their frenzy from some academic scribbler of a few years back.

Economists have become the high priests of a world of money, wealth, and aspirations for material goods. Like the Schoolmen of the Middle Ages, they define for a secular world the relationships between man and man, man and nature, man and society. Their often esoteric and highly complex theories are translated into a folklore understood by millions and into policies adopted by nations. Although their base is usually in the relatively secluded atmosphere of the university, in recent years distinguished economists have served as prime ministers of England, France, Germany, and Italy and as Secretary-General of the United Nations. It would be hard to name another discipline that has exerted as much influence on the modern world.

This was not always the case. Only two hundred years ago

there were no economists known by that name, and economic theory was a branch of moral philosophy. Economics as we know it today hardly existed, and what did exist was called "political economy," indicating that it was part of national policy more than anything else and that it dealt with such matters as taxes, public debts, and foreign trade.

Today, however, economics is the only social science with a generally accepted body of theory whose validity almost every practitioner would accept. It is true that there are many differences of opinion among economists, who sometimes joke about obtaining five different opinions on any topic from any four economists, or about the old professor who asks the same examination questions year after year but changes the answers. There are many disputes among economists, too, but not about the fundamental principles of the science. The disagreements arise over applications, over the proper policies to be adopted in given circumstances, over judgments about the importance of various factors in particular situations.

There is one major exception to this rule — the Marxists, who consider Western economics to be merely an ideological justification of an exploitive system. They believe their own analysis of capitalism to be the correct one, laying bare the flaws that will lead ultimately to the downfall of the Western system. Their contempt for Western economics is reciprocated by the attitude toward Marxism of the Western economists, who consider that doctrine so wrong they don't even bother to read Marx. But while the ideological debate goes on, planners in the East and policy-makers in the West deal with the same economic realities in similar ways, and pragmatism triumphs over ideology.

Economics is a social science, and ideological debates have always been important to its development. This presents a great paradox: some of the most important scientific advances in economics have resulted from political debates over social policy. In this respect economics — like all other social sciences — differs radically from the physical and biological sciences, which have grown step by step from facts and experimental evidence to theory, and from theory to further experiment and more general theories. But the normally slow progress of scientific advance in economics has several times been speeded forward by grand political-philosophical debates. Ideological systems, each with its supporting facts, assumptions, and body of theory, have spawned much that is valuable in economics.

The ideas developed by Adam Smith in the eighteenth century comprised one of those systems, and the theory of markets developed by Smith and his followers represented the first great body of generally accepted principles in modern economics. Challenged by Marx and others in the mid-nineteenth century, this "classical" system and its laissez-faire ideology was remade in the last quarter of the century into a new orthodoxy that prevailed until the 1930's, when John Maynard Keynes almost single-handedly built the modern theory of national income and justified a policy of government intervention in economic affairs. Between these last two developments, a variety of writers laid the foundations for today's welfare policies by criticizing the economic theories of their time. The arguments of each debate led to significant advances in our understanding of the complexities of economic life and to important new generalizations about how economic institutions function.

One of the great themes in the advance of economics, then, has been the interaction of ideology and science. Without the former, the latter could not have evolved. And because scientific economics was forged in the fire of ideological debate, it will always arouse emotions, no matter how "pure" its spokesmen may try to keep it.

A second great theme is the relationship between economic theories and practical problems. People everywhere have sought prosperity and justice, freedom and order, individual betterment and the social good. The quest for these sometimes contradictory goals has always involved choice, and choice is the basic subject matter of economics. One of the truths of economic science is that the greater the difference between the current level of output and the minimum level needed for subsistence, the more numerous are the alternative courses of action and the easier it is to achieve a multiplicity of goals. As society brought a recalcitrant nature more effectively under its control, possible ways and means of organizing and utilizing economic resources became more numerous, and public policy toward economic affairs became more important. With control comes choice, and choice begets policy. The need for policy decisions brought forth the economist, to analyze and advise and to develop a scientific basis for his analysis.

For example, at the close of World War II the American people debated whether or not to institute an extensive program of loans to aid the reconstruction of Europe. The issue would have been strictly academic had not the United States had a large surplus of production above its minimum needs which could be allocated for that purpose. Since the surplus was available, however, economists were called in to advise on how best to mobilize it (whether under public or private auspices), the form it should take (loans or grants, or both), and the uses to which it should be put (consumer goods or machinery, or both). These are economic decisions, involving choices among alternatives.

A third theme in the development of economics is its close relationship to the climate of opinion. A problem is never analyzed in a vacuum. The function of theory is to provide a context in which facts can be systematically organized. But solutions must be practical and, above all, acceptable to the public at large and to its political leaders. If economics is to have any usefulness, the economic theory of an era must be consistent with the other beliefs and concerns of the public. It must provide useful and meaningful results.

Scholars often overlook the importance of public opinion. They seek the origins of ideas in the solid advances made by earlier scholars, tracing an "intellectual genealogy" from one generation of thinkers to another, finding the origins of modern ideas in the Old Testament, Aesop, and the Upanishads. In some respects this is a worthwhile task, for older generations were just as intelligent as we are; it is true more often than not that any good idea has already been conceived by someone else. But in the social sciences, at least, the more meaningful question is not "when did the idea first appear?" but "why is the idea important now?" The answer to the latter question involves the uses to which the idea can be put, the special interests of those who use it, and its consistency with other beliefs of the people affected by it. This climate of opinion is often more important than logical consistency for the development and survival of ideas—more important in the case of economic ideas, perhaps, than of those in any other social science, because of the close relationship between economics and public policy. The economist cannot escape the times in which he lives—they determine the very questions he asks—and every man is, in some respects, his own economist.

A fourth and overriding theme is the development of economics as a science. Over a period of 250 years—a quarter of a millenium—it has developed basic principles about the ways in which markets function, the process of economic growth, the determinants of the level of economic activity, and many other topics. Like any science, economics has evolved a vocabulary of concepts that defines its subject matter, and methods by which hypotheses are tested, modified, and verified. Generations of theorists have developed systematic analyses, demonstrable conclusions, and broad propositions.

Economics is an ever-changing discipline. Partly a product of the great ideological debates over the way human society ought to be organized, it also influences the outcome of those debates. Partly based on a theoretical search for abstract truths, it is also rooted in the realities of public policy and the climate of opinion. Economics is a complex amalgam of scientific theory, political ideology, public policy, and accepted truths.

Yet the advance of the discipline to its present position of pre-eminence among the social sciences could not have taken place without the work of many ordinary and extraordinary individuals. The story of economics is also the story of a Scottish philosopher, a London stockbroker, an Episcopalian minister, a German revolutionist, a Cambridge professor, a Norwegian-American skeptic, and a host of others. The story reflects their personalities and their convictions, their strengths and their weaknesses, their successes and their failures. This book is an account of their work and of the discipline they helped to build, of the interaction among facts, problems, policy, and philosophy in the building process, and of how we have come to think as we do about one of the most important aspects of our lives.

Table of Contents

CHAPTER 1: **ECONOMICS AND THE RISE OF THE MARKET ECONOMY** 1
The Great Transformation 1
Religion and Economic Life 3

CHAPTER 2: **THE EARLY DAYS** 7
The Mercantilists 7
Opposition to Mercantilism 11
The Physiocrats 13
The Economic Liberals 13

CHAPTER 3: **ADAM SMITH** 17
The Philosophical Life 17
The Theoretical Problem: Order, Chaos, and Natural Law 19
Reality: Individualism in English Life 21
The Solution: Economic Freedom 23
The Self-Adjusting Market 25
Two Qualifications 27
Economic Growth 28
Smith's Achievement 30

CHAPTER 4: **CLASSICAL ECONOMICS** 32
England's Reaction to the French Revolution 33
Malthus and the Theory of Population 34
Ricardo and Economic Growth 37
The International Economy 40
Say's Law of Markets 41
Bentham and Interventionist Liberalism 45

CHAPTER 5: **SOCIALISM AND KARL MARX** 49
Socialism and the Climate of Opinion 50
Robert Owen, Utopian 51
Karl Marx, Revolutionary 53
The Breakdown of Capitalism 55
The Marxist Vision 57
Was Marx Wrong? 59

CHAPTER 6: **THE PHILOSOPHY OF INDIVIDUALISM** 61
The Philosophy 62
Individualism and the Law 64
The Folklore of Individualism 66
Results of Individualism 68
The Limitations of Individualism 71

CHAPTER 7: **NEOCLASSICAL ECONOMICS** 72
Marginal Utility and Individual Welfare 72
Economic Justice 75
Prosperity and Depression 76
The Ideology of Capitalism 79
Scientific Advances 81

CHAPTER 8: **THE FAMILY OF MAN** 84
Papal Economics 85
Philosophers of the Welfare State 87
Veblen, Commons, and the New Deal 90

CHAPTER 9: **THE KEYNESIAN REVOLUTION** 98
John Maynard Keynes 99
The Climate of Opinion in the Mid-1930's 101
The General Theory of Employment 105
The Meaning of Keynesian Economics 107

CHAPTER 10: **ECONOMIC PLANNING** 109
Planning in the Soviet Union 110
The Theory of Planning 115
Planning in Underdeveloped Nations 117

CHAPTER 11: **WILL CAPITALISM SURVIVE?**   121
Joseph Schumpeter, Pessimist   121
Economic Growth After World War II   123
The Changing Economic System   127
Changing Technology   132
The Challenges Ahead   136

Suggestions for Further Reading   **138**

Index of Names   **145**

Economics
and the
Rise of the Market Economy

THE GREAT TRANSFORMATION

Because the modern market economy is such an intimate part of our way of life, most of us do not realize that it is a relatively recent development. The organization of economic life around an interrelated system of markets—markets which adjust prices, output, and incomes to an impersonal system of market forces—did not emerge on a large scale until after the Middle Ages, that is, from the fifteenth century onward. Prior to that time the bulk of Europe's population lived in an economy largely based upon a social system of rights and obligations rather than on an acquisitive, profit-oriented economy of buying and selling.

This transformation of society and its economy was observed by contemporaries. Thomas Becon, an English cleric of the mid-sixteenth century, for example, decried the growing materialism of his era and inveighed against "greedy gentlemen, which are sheepmongers and graziers" who "study for their own private commodity." Thomas Wilson, writing fifty years later, noted how even the aristocracy was affected by the change:

The gentlemen, which were wont to addict themselves to warres, are now for the most part growen to become good husbands and know well how to improve their lands to the uttermost as the farmer or countryman, so that they take their farmes into their handes as the leases expire, and eyther till themselves or else lett them out to those who will give most.

Becon and Wilson observed what many others of the time could also see. The traditional pattern, in which each person was born to a definite place and fulfilled a definite function all his life, was passing away. The peasant, long accustomed to providing services for his lord and paying him a portion of his agricultural output, increasingly paid money rents and sold a portion of his product in order to get the money to do so. More than ever before, the lord of the manor, or estate, used his rents to buy what he needed, and the more progressive landowners began to produce readily marketable products like wool. Others gradually raised the rents charged their tenants, who were forced to similarly orient their crops toward marketable products. Middlemen traders increased in number, wealth, and importance as a result of the growing market.

The Middle Ages—that era from the breakdown of the ancient Roman Empire to the mid-fifteenth century—were not without trade, commerce, and markets, but the trade was in large part a long-distance and interregional trade in luxury products consumed by the nobility and the wealthy. Peasant communities, rural and largely self-sufficient, produced a surplus paid to the lord in products, in labor, and sometimes in cash. This surplus was the basis for purchases of luxuries by the aristocracy—things like fine textiles, metal products, wine, and other items of the "good life." A dual economy grew up, comprising the peasant village on the one hand and the commercial town on the other. It was a regulated economy of organized groups such as manor, town, and guild rather than one which operated through free decisions freely negotiated. In its fundamental structure it was much like the economic system that prevailed throughout the rest of the civilized world westward to the Near and Middle East, southeast Asia, and the Far East.

Then, in the fifteenth century, the great transformation of Europe to a market economy began. The geographical discoveries of the fifteenth and sixteenth centuries opened up tremendous opportunities for trade and commerce and set in motion a large flow of capital into Europe in the form of gold and silver treasures from both the New World and the East. The rise of national states largely destroyed the political power of two bulwarks of the old order, the nobility and the Church. New methods of warfare used by the emerging rulers, featuring paid infantries and large navies, required money and administration: national tax systems emerged, and a flow of purchasing power from taxpayer through government and back to the public further stimulated the growth of markets. Cities like London and Amsterdam became centers of commerce; they looked overseas for their profits and expansion, and they were supported by governments eager to increase the tax base by expanding the wealth of the nation.

The new economy generated new attitudes. The medieval man, accustomed to thinking and acting in traditional ways, gave way to a new market-oriented man who would sink or swim by virtue of his individual decisions. The man who succeeded was the man who saved, who plowed his profits back into his enterprise, who calculated prices and costs carefully, who took risks in order to make gains. In particular, there was little place for the attitudes of the old nobility, who set great store by blood lineage and the traditions of feudal warfare and jousting. The future lay with commercial profits and commercial wealth.

The new economy also generated the study of economics. The developing market orientation of production and distribution led to new relationships between man and society and between man and man, with all the ethical issues that those relationships imply. The morality of the new economic order had to be carefully analyzed and accepted rules for ethical behavior devised. Theologians became the first "economists."

RELIGION AND ECONOMIC LIFE

The theologians were concerned with reconstructing the ethical basis of economic life. The older medieval point of view had subordinated economic life to both individual salvation and the needs of society as a whole. Theologians had argued that earthly life was merely a prelude to eternity, and moral laws had to prevail in all aspects of human endeavor. This meant that in all human relationships, including the economic, the individual had to keep the law of God continually in mind. The Church knew that man must eat and clothe and house himself, that the ordinary functions of production and distribution had to be carried on; but those functions had to be placed in proper perspective — salvation was the proper business of life, and one must never forget it. Seeking wealth for its own sake was sinful, for it took one's attention away from salvation and pursuit of the moral life.

The economic attitudes embodied in the orthodox moral philosophy of the Middle Ages were summed up in a famous parable. A monk on a pilgrimage to Rome purchased a silver chalice for his cathedral. Traveling back to Germany with a band of merchants, he showed them the vessel and told what he had paid for it. The merchants congratulated him on his purchase, telling him that he had bought it for far less than its true value, and laughed that an unworldly monk could drive a better bargain than any of them. Horrified, the monk left immediately, made his way back to Rome, and paid the seller of the chalice enough to make up the fair price. It was the only moral thing to do.

Such attitudes may have been consistent with an economy of customary prices and accepted economic relationships, but they were out of tune with the success-oriented, profit-motivated behavior of the market economy. They may have been appropriate to people concerned with eternal salvation, but they did not suit people who sought material wealth and success. They may have worked in a society organized in stable groups, but they were incompatible with an individualistic social order and a desire to rise in wealth and status.

The rise of a market economy created a moral dilemma for the new man of the early modern era. On the one hand, the ethical teachings of his religion told him that all men were brothers and that each individual was morally responsible for others. These ideas were found in the Old Testament story of Cain and Abel and in the New Testament parable of the Good Samaritan, to give only two widely known examples. On the other hand, survival and success in a market economy required that each person try to outreach, outsmart, and overcome his fellows. Rivalry, not brotherhood, was the necessary mode of behavior, and the principle of *caveat emptor*—"let the buyer beware"—prevailed. Market relationships were impersonal and transient compared with the permanent and face-to-face relationships of an unchanging rural village. Men were judged more by their success in acquiring wealth than by the morality of their behavior.

This moral dilemma—the conflict between salvation and success—was an important factor in setting the stage for the Reformation. It was hard for an urban merchant to believe that his mode of living was less proper than that of others. It was difficult for him to understand that the competition necessary for his survival was antagonistic to the moral law, that the single-minded pursuit of profit which was fundamental to his very livelihood was frowned upon by the divines. So doubts arose. Were the theologians right in their teachings about the modes of conduct required for salvation? After all, they were only men like everyone else and therefore subject to human error. What did the Bible itself say about these matters? Such questions led inevitably to the Protestant heresy—doubt of the infallibility of the Church and a desire to go directly to the Bible as the repository of God's law, without the priest as intermediary.

The theological arguments of the Reformation are of little interest to us here, but out of them came a new economic ethic that gave the profit-motivated market economy its moral letters of credit.

Underlying the new morality was the idea that God in his infinite wisdom had intended a place on earth for each individual, through which the individual could work out his destiny. This place, or "calling," had to be sought and found by personal soul-searching, and once found it had to be diligently pursued. Salvation was earned by hard work in one's calling, and any calling — even that of the merchant — was equal in merit to any other in the eyes of God. Worldly success indicated that a man had found his calling and that God had smiled upon him. Avoid idleness, temptation, and luxury . . . work hard and save. These were the prescriptions for ethical behavior hammered out during a half-century of religious controversy, sermonizing, and polemics. They fitted the needs of the growing urban middle class and promoted the hard work and capital accumulation that led to economic expansion.

By the eighteenth century the new economic ethic had lost much of its religious sanction and had become an almost universal way of life. That American sage, Benjamin Franklin, stated it in the form of aphorisms, which were repeated endlessly to generations of young people:

> Early to bed, early to rise, makes a man
> healthy, wealthy, and wise.

> The sound of your hammer at five in the
> morning, or at nine at night,
> heard by a creditor, makes him easy six
> months longer.

> What maintains one vice would bring up
> two children.

The new ethic was the basis of a secular and materialistic value system that has dominated the climate of opinion in Western Europe and North America ever since.

But even though attitudes changed and the accepted goals of individual action became heavily materialistic, a moral problem remained. Was it true that economic failure meant unworthiness, that success and salvation were synonymous? Did not the individual have a responsibility to others that went beyond merely meeting one's contractual obligations in the marketplace? Had the monk been correct in returning to Rome to pay the merchant more for the chalice than his bargain called for?

The problem arises because of the inherent conflict between an ethical principle — all men are brothers — and the competitive rivalry of the market economy expressed in the legal principle of *caveat emptor* —

"let the buyer beware." The ethical principle requires the individual to take responsibility for others, while the legal principle calls for the individual to look out only for himself.

This moral dilemma has puzzled philosophers and ecclesiastics from the sixteenth century onward. Attempted solutions appeared in the religious controversies of the sixteenth century, in the eighteenth-century philosophy of *noblesse oblige,* in the writings of nineteenth-century socialists, and in the welfare legislation of the twentieth century. Present in all these approaches to the problem is a belief that the social system should not allow an individual to be crushed and destroyed by the operation of impersonal market forces. But the dilemma of "moral man and immoral society" remains, and economists must be, in part, moral philosophers, while philosophers must also deal with economic issues.

2

The Early Days

Practical men will often argue over the most esoteric of subjects, for policy decisions sometimes rest upon the most intricate of theories. One of these debates took place during the eighteenth century, and from it emerged the foundations of modern economics. The question at issue was the ultimate source of national wealth, which some saw in trade, others in agriculture and the natural forces of life, and still others in human labor. Although the issue may seem at first glance to be devoid of practical significance, the whole range of government economic policy depended on the outcome.

THE MERCANTILISTS

The mercantilists were the first to take the field. These men were concerned with the national states that developed during the sixteenth and seventeenth centuries. They faced two different but related problems, one internal and one external.

The domestic problem was one of unity. National power had to be built from the localism of the Middle Ages. For the economy this meant a unified coinage and monetary system, a national system of weights and measures, elimination of internal tolls on roads and rivers, and a national system of taxes and tariffs. These institutions, which today we take for granted, were slowly forged by national rulers against the opposition of feudal lords who tried to keep as much control as possible over the economy of their regions. The building of a national economy was predicated on the growing political power of the kings against the great nobles.

In this struggle the kings found natural allies in several places. First in importance were the rising commercial interests of the towns and cities. Merchants benefited from the widened trade made possible by a unified economy in which local barriers to commerce were reduced. In turn, the merchants augmented the kings' power by helping to finance the armies needed to subordinate the nobility. The interests of kings and merchants further coincided in that both benefited from expanded foreign trade. Merchants earned profits from trade with the newly opened lands in Asia and the New World. To the extent that the merchants of one country dominated trade with another area, profits would flow to the homeland and domestic manufacturers would be stimulated by the export market. The kings gained from the tariff revenues derived from large trade, from the sale of trade monopolies, from the development of strategic military industries and personnel — shipbuilding and ship supplies, sailors and captains — and from the general economic growth that provided a firm economic base for national power. One of the basic goals of national policy, therefore, became the development of commerce and the growth of power in international affairs.

A second group allied with the kings were the smaller landowners, who looked to the kings as a counterweight to the powers of the barons. This group was more interested in commercial agriculture than in warfare, jousts, and family power and wanted the kings to maintain order and promote the growing markets from which they profited. They knew that as the power of the kings increased vis-à-vis the great lords, their own wealth and power in local affairs would also increase.

Two other groups emerged from the rising market economy and national states. One was the legal profession, whose members were needed to interpret and define the vastly complicated economic relationships that developed out of free association and private contract in the market environment. Old and familiar legal relationships were being replaced by new ones, and lawyers were needed to systematize them. The second group comprised public administrators and the court. Although small in numbers, these two groups were of great strategic importance. A "white-collar" superstructure, allied with and dependent upon business and government, supported the policies designed to strengthen unity and power.

Out of the political-economic alliances among crown, merchants, gentry, and professional people emerged economic policies designed to unify the nation under a single strong ruler, develop its military and naval strength, and increase its wealth through both domestic production and foreign trade. These and the theories underlying them have come to be called *mercantilism*. It was the first systematic body of modern economic thought.

One of the clearest statements of mercantilist policy was made by Phillip von Hornick (1638–1712), an Austrian civil servant writing for a backward country constantly threatened by the Turks. He wrote in 1684 a widely read tract called *Austria Over All, If She Only Will*, listing "nine principal rules of national economy":

> To inspect the country's soil with the greatest care, and not to leave the agricultural possibilities or a single corner or clod of earth unconsidered . . . all commodities found in a country, which cannot be used in their natural state, should be worked up within the country . . . attention should be given to the population, that it may be as large as the country can support . . . gold and silver once in the country are under no circumstances to be taken out for any purpose . . . the inhabitants should make every effort to get along with their domestic products . . . [foreign commodities] should be obtained not for gold or silver, but in exchange for other domestic wares . . . and should be imported in unfinished form, and worked up within the country . . . opportunities should be sought night and day for selling the country's superfluous goods to these foreigners in manufactured form . . . no importation should be allowed under any circumstances of which there is a sufficient supply of suitable quality at home.

These basic policies of nationalism, self-sufficiency, and national power were adopted in varying degrees by all the states of Europe. Manufacturing was encouraged by subsidies, special privileges, patents, and monopolies. Foreign trade was stimulated by acquisition of colonies and efforts to keep wages down and regulated by tariffs, navigation laws, and trade restrictions. Agriculture was fostered by a variety of policies: in England imports of food were taxed in order to keep out foreign competition, while in France exports of agricultural products were taxed in order to keep domestic production at home. In particular, the munitions industries were promoted—guns, gunpowder, ships, and ship supplies.

In England, where trade quickly became the basis for increased wealth and national power, a great deal of emphasis was placed on expansion of the money supply as a stimulus to economic growth. In those days of limited markets and inadequate purchasing power, one of the barriers to economic growth was a lack of both hard cash in the hands of consumers and credit available for businessmen. Kings often borrowed, too, and they would similarly benefit from readily available cash and credit and from low interest rates. Modern banking was only in its infancy, and the availability of money and credit depended very heavily on the cash available — and that meant gold and silver coins. It was inevitable, then, that monetary policy was a major concern of the mercantilist economists. Basically, they favored what we would call an "easy money" policy — plenty of money to stimulate trade and keep interest rates down. On the other hand, they had to keep inflationary pressures in check, for two reasons: (1) rising prices created difficulties for the workers and the poor, because wage rates tended to lag behind price increases, and political unrest would therefore follow; (2) rising prices would reduce foreign demand for domestic manufactures and ultimately result in worsened economic conditions at home.

Domestic and international economic policies, therefore, became closely intertwined, and the English mercantilists were quick to realize that the world economy was a web of interconnections. Hard experience as well as sharp analysis taught them that if the domestic money supply and purchasing power expanded more rapidly than the supply of goods available for sale, domestic prices would rise, imports would increase, and exports would fall. The fall in exports and rise in imports would then result in an export of gold and silver to make up for the "unfavorable" balance of trade. This in turn would reduce the money supply at home and cause the domestic economy to languish. These relationships were soon well understood, and a cardinal tenet of the mercantilists was encouragement of a "favorable" balance of trade. If exports exceeded imports, they argued, gold and silver would enter the country, plenty of money would be available, economic growth would be stimulated, and national wealth would grow.

It should not be assumed that mercantilism was everywhere the same. There were great differences between countries. In France, for example, where luxury products like silks and linens, tapestries, furniture, and wine were of major importance, close regulation of the quality of goods was emphasized. Under the leadership of Jean Baptiste Colbert (1619–1683), minister of finance for more than twenty years during the reign of Louis XIV, national guilds were set up to regulate the major industries. Only craftsmen who were guild members could operate, and they were subject to the regulations of the national organization. The royal power was strong enough to enforce the regulations effectively, and the guilds remained powerful until the French Revolution at the end of the eighteenth century.

In England, by contrast, regulation of domestic industry was not successful because the government was never strong enough to administer it effectively. English mercantilism was devoted primarily to expansion of trade and encouragement of manufactures. One result of this situation was that the medieval guilds disintegrated, especially when cloth production developed in rural areas, and industrial processes were far freer of restrictions than were those of France. When the Industrial Revolution began, this absence of guilds gave English industry a long head start over that of France and the other continental countries which had copied the French example.

Nor was there always agreement on policies within nations. Popular revulsion in England against government grants of monopoly to individuals and companies was so great that in 1601 Queen Elizabeth herself had to appear before Parliament to quell the objections and promise reforms. Two years later, in the famous "Case of Monopolies," the courts decided in a path-breaking decision that even monopoly grants by the Crown were subject to the common-law prohibitions on restraint of trade. Parliament finally prohibited government grants of monopoly in 1624, completing the legal foundations on which American antitrust laws are based.

The mercantilists argued that real wealth was produced by labor — by human effort in general — but it was felt that this wealth would not be realized unless trade and commerce were encouraged, unless exchange of goods enabled producers to make a profit. For this reason they emphasized the growth of trade and commerce as the key to increased national wealth, and expansion of the money supply as the key to increased trade. To the question, "What is the source of the wealth of nations?" the mercantilists gave the first answer: "Commerce."

In many respects they were right. In the sixteenth and seventeenth centuries the most powerful nations of Europe were those that had developed their international and overseas trade to the greatest extent. Trade seemed to stimulate both manufacturing and agriculture and to bring prosperity, wealth, and power to the entire nation. Mercantilist doctrines had a common-sense validity derived from what people could see going on around them.

OPPOSITION TO MERCANTILISM

By the middle of the eighteenth century the mercantilists' preoccupation with trade and national power had begun to grate on some of the economic interests of the growing market economy. Mercantilist policies were fine for the great merchants and financiers who operated in the international economy; the basic goals of national power suited the kings; and government administrators and courtiers were often able to benefit substantially, either directly or through bribes, from government grants of special economic privilege. But the economy became more varied as it grew, and both agricultural and industrial interests were increasingly coming to find that mercantilist policies were not in their best interest. The policies were subjected to substantial criticism, and the theories on which they were based were questioned.

Small businessmen, in particular, felt hemmed in by the monopolistic privileges granted to a few big financiers, and both they and the smaller farmers resented the taxes imposed to maintain a national power alien to their individual interests. A classic example is the issue of "taxation without representation" in Britain's American colonies. When the French and Indian Wars ended in 1765, the western frontiers of the colonies were relatively safe for colonization and development, and the colonists were well aware of the fact that much of their economic future lay in the West. But the British government, long committed to development of the fur trade and favoring the interests of the Hudson's Bay Company, had prohibited settlement beyond the Allegheny Mountains. Troops were stationed in the colonies to protect the frontier and enforce the prohibition, which protected the colonists from the Indians before 1765 but which restricted colonial economic growth after the frontier was pacified. To make matters worse, taxes on legal documents and tea were imposed in the colonies to pay for the troops, who were sometimes quartered in the homes of colonials: the colonists had to support the very troops who were protecting the interests of Englishmen against themselves! One wonders what attitude the colonists would have taken had the tax revenues been used to open the frontier rather than close it.

The case of the American colonies, where the issue became political and helped lead to the American Revolution, was a striking example of opposition to mercantilist policies. In Europe, however, a debate about purely economic issues arose. Was it true that economic expansion and growth was best achieved through regulation and direction? Would not better results be achieved in a free economy unhampered by the directing force of a mercantilist government? The debate over these questions was particularly strong in France and England.

In France, government regulation of production was so detailed as to specify the required number of threads per inch in the manufacture of cloth. There was a multiplicity of taxes and tolls, and regulation of imports and exports was strict. Yet the nobility was exempt from taxation while substantial levies were imposed on peasants and independent farmers. Moreover, the government was corrupt and inefficient—indeed, this condition probably made the system workable: the regulations and taxes could often be evaded by judicious bribes or clever evasions. The situation was so bad that one government inspector of trademarks, Vincent de Gournay (1712–1759), disenchanted with mercantilist regulation, is reputed to have originated the famous phrase, "*laissez faire, laissez passer,*" or "free enterprise, free trade."

THE PHYSIOCRATS

The most important French antimercantilists called themselves *physiocrats*. Their leader was François Quesnay (1694–1774), court physician to Louis XV. Quesnay disagreed with the mercantilist assumption that wealth originated in industry and trade. He argued that only agriculture, by virtue of the life-giving aspects of nature, could produce a surplus over and above the effort invested in production. Quesnay then went on in his famous *Economic Table* of 1758 to show how the surplus from agriculture flowed through the entire economy in the form of rent, wages, and purchases, supporting all the social classes as it went. Two policy conclusions stemmed from his analysis: (1) regulation of trade and industry impeded economic development by hindering the flow of income and commodities on which the economy depended; (2) all taxes should be paid by landowners (as distinguished from farmers) partly because they were not productive and partly because their luxurious way of living distorted the flow of income.

Quesnay had been greatly impressed by the discovery of the circulation of blood in the human body and likened the circulation of money and products to that biological process. He believed profoundly that all wealth came ultimately from the life-giving process created by God. A strong believer in the supremacy of natural law, he felt that a regime of economic freedom would be both beneficial and self-regulating.

Another physiocrat, Jacques Turgot (1727–1781), rose to be minister of finance. In two short years he introduced a variety of antifeudal and antimercantilist reforms and was supported by the king, but opposition from the nobility forced him out of office. Even the "absolute" ruler of France was unable to push through reforms over the opposition of the nobility, and a few years later the old regime was swept away.[1]

All the physiocrats agreed on one basic proposition, that wealth came ultimately from the land. Only land contained the life-giving forces of nature derived from God. Manufacturing could change only the form of wealth derived from nature, and commerce could change only its location and ownership. Land alone could produce a surplus. This was the second major theory of the source of wealth.

THE ECONOMIC LIBERALS

The physiocratic interlude was short, although its influence hung on even in the United States, where a long line of statesmen from

[1]During the Revolution another prominent physiocrat, Pierre du Pont de Nemours, emigrated to the United States, where he stayed for several years. In 1802 his son founded a small gunpowder factory near Wilmington, Delaware, the beginning of the great Du Pont chemical enterprise.

Jefferson to Lincoln were convinced that the nation's future depended on encouraging the small farmer. Far more important was the rise of economic liberalism. From small beginnings in the late seventeenth and early eighteenth centuries, it became the mainstream of economic thought in the nineteenth century and lives on today as the classic capitalist ideology.

The early economic liberals—those who advocated the doctrine before it was systematized by Adam Smith in the latter part of the eighteenth century—first attacked restrictions on international trade and fought for an end to tariffs, monopolies, and regulations. They based their argument on the social theory that individual motives, however selfish they might be, resulted in benefits to society as a whole.

The first important economic liberal in England was Dudley North (1641–1691) whose *Discourses Upon Trade* was published anonymously in the year of his death. Because North was a wealthy merchant and landowner who became a treasury official, it is understandable that he was cautious in publishing an attack on the nationalistic policies of mercantilism. His book made a strong case for free trade and attacked the mercantilist assumption that a favorable balance of trade was necessarily desirable. People trade, he argued, because it is advantageous to both parties, promoting specialization, division of labor, and the increase of wealth. Regulation interfered with these benefits by reducing and restricting trade and inevitably reduced real wealth.

North's argument was supported by the philosopher and historian David Hume (1711–1776), who in 1752 pointed out that an automatic economic process would cause any favorable balance of trade to disappear: a surplus of exports would be paid for by imports of gold and silver, which would increase the money supply and cause prices to rise, which in turn would cause a decline in exports until exports and imports were in balance. It was therefore impossible for mercantilist policy to continuously maintain both a favorable balance of trade and imports of gold and silver.

The logic of North and Hume made mincemeat of the mercantilist arguments for regulation of foreign trade. According to Hume, the policies would not work, and North showed that the results would be undesirable if they *did* work.

In the meantime, a fascinating, popular, and controversial book had appeared in 1704, a doggerel poem called *The Fable of the Bees*, written by Bernard de Mandeville (1670–1733), a Dutch doctor who had emigrated to England. The poem's basic argument was that advances in civilization were the result of man's vices, not his virtues. Progress came from the selfish interests of the individual—his desire for ease and comfort, luxury and pleasure—not from any natural propensity to work hard and save or from benevolent concern for others. Prosperity and economic growth would be increased by giving free play to the selfish motives of the individual, limited only by the maintenance of justice. The vice of selfishness would spur each person on to maximize his gains and thereby add to the wealth of the nation:

> Thus Vice nurs'd Ingenuity,
> Which joined with Time and Industry,
> Had carry'd Life's Conveniencies,
> Its real Pleasures, Comforts, Ease,
> To such a Height, the very Poor
> Liv'd better than the Rich before,
> And nothing could be added more.

The book was suppressed by an embarrassed government, with the full support of the guardians of morality. Yet, together with the theory of natural economic adjustments described by North and Hume, the selfish motives lauded by Mandeville became the basis of the next great economic theory—economic liberalism.

The economic liberals of the eighteenth century found the source of wealth in neither trade nor agriculture but in human labor. It was through individual effort, they argued, that production takes place and the wherewithal to satisfy human needs is provided. Nature produces few materials that man can use in natural form: almost all natural products must be transformed by human effort before they can satisfy man's wants. Without productive effort, natural products are worthless.

This labor theory of value emphasized that the production of wealth had as its ultimate purpose the satisfaction of human wants. Wealth could not be considered an end in itself, nor was the aggrandizement of national power its proper end. Wealth *was* wealth because it made people better off. The production of wealth, furthermore, depended not on the fertility of the soil or on favorable trade balances but on the individual incentives of ordinary people. Man's motive for work was his need to provide himself with food, clothing, shelter, and comforts. The greater the incentive to work, the greater would be the production of wealth and the faster would mankind move toward a more abundant society.

John Locke (1632–1704), the English philosopher, tied together labor, production of wealth, and private property, and in doing so he made the institution of property one of the cornerstones of national wealth. By adding his labor to natural resources, man added part of himself to the final product, making the product "his" to use or consume. Both wealth and private property were simultaneously produced by human labor. In Locke's words:

God hath given the world to men in common. . . . Yet every man has a property in his own person. The labour of his body and the work of his hands we may say are properly his. Whatsoever, then, he removes out of the state that nature hath provided and left it in, he hath mixed his labour with, and joined to it something that is his own, and thereby makes it his property.

Later economic liberals made much of these connections between labor, wealth, and property. They argued that the first requisite for national economic growth was the protection of private property, for unless the right to property was sustained the incentive to work was reduced, and the production of wealth would fall.

A favorite illustration of this principle was a comparison of the wealth of the English and the poverty of the Turks. In ancient times, liberals pointed out, the domain of the Turk was the wealthiest in the world, with flourishing cities, prosperous agriculture, large exports, and world-famous manufactures. But a despotic and arbitrary government seized wealth without justification, imposed confiscatory taxes, and operated both justice and government through a system of bribery. These actions brought an end to prosperity. The Turk languished in poverty thereafter, unwilling to work, to produce, or to accumulate capital because he knew it would be seized or destroyed by a corrupt government. Happy and prosperous England, on the other hand, was growing in wealth because individual initiative was protected by a rule of law that preserved for the individual the wealth he produced and saved. Justice was evenhanded, not arbitrary. The sanctity of private contracts was preserved, and no property could be taken for public use without just compensation. Whatever the individual earned was his to use as he alone saw fit — within the limits of legality and decency. According to the economic liberal, the functions of government were few: protection of property, maintenance of justice, and national defense. The economy would operate within this framework without additional aid or regulation. Individual incentives would produce national wealth.

There were many variations on this theme. Some economic liberals would grant broader powers to the national government, others put more stress on the strength of individual incentives and competition, still others on the operation of supply and demand in free markets. But all agreed on the need to free individual initiative from the limitations imposed by mercantilist restrictions, on the importance of work in producing wealth, and on the necessity of protecting and preserving property rights as the cornerstone of economic policy.

3

Adam Smith

Adam Smith was the greatest of the economic liberals. A philosopher and college professor, he is considered today to be the founder of modern economics. Strangely enough, in his own lifetime he was known primarily for his writings in philosophy, rather than economics, and had little influence on public policy. He cultivated his academic garden, and the flowers did not bloom until later.

THE PHILOSOPHICAL LIFE

Smith was born in Kirkaldy, Scotland, in 1723, a few months after his father's death. His childhood was quiet and uneventful, and at fourteen he entered the University of Glasgow. He did well enough to win a scholarship to Oxford, where he spent six years, dismayed by what he considered to be the low level of intellectual activity and the immorality of his fellow students. In 1751 he went to the University of Edinburgh to lecture, and the following year he became professor of logic at Glasgow when an opening suddenly appeared. Luck seemed to follow the young professor, for the next year the professorship of moral philosophy — Smith's favorite subject — became vacant, and he was appointed to that post. He lectured on ethics and his book *The*

Theory of Moral Sentiments was published in 1759. To the modern reader it seems old-fashioned but interesting. Its basic idea is that ethical systems develop by a natural process out of individual personal relationships—a view that reflects the eighteenth-century interest in natural law. The individual decides that certain actions are proper or improper by observing the reactions of others to his behavior. A social consensus then develops, approving those patterns of behavior that benefit both society and the individual. The process amounts to an early "other-directed" theory of human action. The book was an immediate success and caught on well with the intelligentsia. Smith's reputation grew, and students even came from the Continent to study under him. He set to work writing a book on economics and began lecturing on "Police, Justice, Revenue and Arms" at the university.

Then came his greatest stroke of luck, but one that he had thoroughly earned. Charles Townshend, the politician who later as Chancellor of the Exchequer was responsible for the tea tax and other taxes that helped bring on the American Revolution, married a wealthy widow and acquired a teen-age stepson. An appropriate education for the young Duke of Buccleuch became important, and Townshend resolved to get the best. He had been very impressed by Adam Smith's book—and by the popular and critical esteem in which it was held—so he approached the forty-year-old philosopher to take a position as the young Duke's tutor. To the surprise of his friends, including the philosopher David Hume, Smith accepted the post: it involved a three-year sojourn in France and a lifetime pension of three hundred pounds a year (about fifteen hundred dollars, a large sum in those days).

Much of the time in France was spent in Toulouse, where Smith, bored, began writing his book on economics. Later, in Paris, Smith met the leading physiocrats Quesnay and Turgot and discussed their doctrines.

Returning to Scotland, Smith lived on his pension and continued writing his book. His friends wondered when it would be finished, for he seemed to work on it interminably. Finally, in 1776, *An Inquiry Into the Nature and Causes of the Wealth of Nations* was published.[1] The book was successful but not popular. Although it was read and appreciated by some, the general public ignored it. William Pitt seems to have based some of his tax proposals of the late 1780's on Smith's ideas, but it was not until twenty years after Smith's death that a new generation of writers, intent on building a new science of political economy, established Smith as the founder of their science and a major genius.

---

[1]Other important events occurred in 1776. Jeremy Bentham's *Fragment on Government* and Richard Price's *On Civil Liberty* were published, and Parliament rejected a bill that would have provided for universal male suffrage. "Discontent" continued in the American colonies.

In the meantime, the author returned to Scotland and in 1778 was appointed commissioner of the customs, a post his father had held. His death in 1790 passed almost unnoticed by his contemporaries.

Adam Smith did not lead a spectacular life. As a child of three he was kidnaped by gypsies for a few hours, and as a grown man he was once confronted briefly by a robber but otherwise he had few adventures. Typically, he was absent-minded. Strolling in his garden at Kirkaldy one Sunday morning, wearing a dressing gown and lost in concentration, he took a wrong turn down the turnpike and walked fifteen miles to Dunfermline before his thoughts were interrupted by the church bells. But despite the colorless personality of its author, the *Wealth of Nations* is a great book because of its theme of individualism and its influence on later economists.

THE THEORETICAL PROBLEM: ORDER, CHAOS, AND NATURAL LAW

One of the great problems of social philosophy in the eighteenth century was how social order emerges out of the potential chaos of an individualistic society. In the Middle Ages, under the influence of religious doctrine, it was assumed that a universal law, ordained by God, underlay both natural and social order and that the law could be discerned by "right reason." But the Renaissance introduced a rational, scientific point of view, and the Reformation weakened religious explanations. In the seventeenth and eighteenth centuries the development of science and mathematics greatly strengthened naturalistic rather than theological explanations and led to theories in which natural forces were sufficient to explain events. In many fields of intellectual inquiry, scientists, philosophers, and political theorists were engaged in creating a new climate of opinion within which man could understand the world around him.

The greatest advance in the natural sciences was made by the English physicist Isaac Newton (1642 – 1727). His *Mathematical Principles of Natural Philosophy* (1687) pictured a mechanical universe operating under the influence of basic natural laws of motion, gravitation, and conservation of energy to achieve a balance of forces, or equilibrium, in which all objects had their proper place. A great theory, it was proved to the public by the return of Halley's Comet in 1759, just as Edmund Halley had predicted after calculating its orbit in 1682.

Other sciences were similarly developed on the basis of natural laws. Robert Boyle discovered in 1660 that the volume of a gas varies inversely with the pressure. Antoine Lavoisier proved the law of conservation of matter through quantitative chemical analysis: matter changes its form but not its quantity. In biology, William Harvey discovered and demonstrated the circulation of blood, and in the eighteenth century the regularity of nature was emphasized when plant and animal forms were systematically classified in interrelated groups by biology and zoology.

The social sciences shared in the emphasis on natural law, regularity, and equilibrium. The thinking of Hugo Grotius (1583–1645), the Dutch legal theorist and father of modern international law, is typical of the early development of these ideas as applied to the social system. Grotius postulated that men are inherently social beings and cannot survive without some form of social organization. Therefore, he argued, certain minimal conditions, or natural laws of society, must be realized if human society is to exist. Grotius listed the natural conditions of society as security of property, good faith and fair dealing, and correspondence between individual efforts and rewards.

The problem of a natural social order arose because of the changing structure of society in the seventeenth and eighteenth centuries. In medieval times each person had his place as part of one or more organized groups, each with its defined rights and obligations. Lord and peasant, miller and priest, were each part of a village community, and each had his duties and obligations to others. Craftsman and merchant were members of guilds and citizens of towns, and each had his place and function, at least in theory if not always in practice. When this social system of organized groups and established rights and duties broke down, what was to take its place? Could society function at all when composed only of individual units—and selfish ones at that—following their own bent and trying to outreach each other? How could social harmony be achieved in this environment of individualistic chaos?

Political philosophers wrestled with these questions, because the whole governmental structure and its rationale depended on the answer. Out of the political dialogue, particularly in England, emerged the classical theory of democracy. Men are inherently selfish, it was argued, and they institute governments in order to protect their natural rights as individuals—life, liberty, and ownership of property. A supporter of absolute monarchy, Thomas Hobbes (1588–1679), argued for absolutism on the grounds that the stronger the power exercised by the sovereign, the more successful would be the social restraint on the selfish, combative element in human nature. John Locke (1632–1704), on the other hand, argued that order and freedom were compatible: men institute governments to avoid chaos and preserve their natural rights, but absolute power is granted to no one. The function of the state is to enforce the laws of nature and punish infractions of them, and the laws of nature are superior even to acts of the state. Within this structure, Locke said, individual action could be given free play.

To these foundations of democratic theory Locke and his followers added the theory of majority rule: the interests of all men in preservation of order were essentially similar, and the best method of determining the common good was decision-making by a majority of all men. Only the individual could know what was in his own best interest, and while a single person could be wrong in any one instance, it was highly unlikely that the consensus of a large group would be seriously in error.

Finally, the Jewish philosopher Baruch Spinoza (1632–1677) added the last link to the liberal political philosophy: checks and balances within the government were necessary in order to temper power with justice.

By the early years of the eighteenth century the political philosophers had developed a theory of liberal democracy based on natural-law precepts. An analysis of the economy in similar terms was next on the agenda. Toward the middle of the century there were several unsuccessful attempts by a variety of writers to produce systematic treatises on the natural laws of economic life and their relationship to individual freedom and government action. It was to this problem in social philosophy that Adam Smith directed his efforts. The *Wealth of Nations* was the result.

REALITY: INDIVIDUALISM IN ENGLISH LIFE

England in the eighteenth century was an open society in almost every area of life outside of politics. The imaginative common man could seize excellent opportunities to rise. Individual initiative and innovation were becoming mass phenomena. In the practical and fine arts, it was the golden age of English pottery and of the great furniture makers such as Chippendale and Sheraton. English painting reached its greatest heights with Gainsborough, Reynolds, Romney, and others, and Handel composed his great oratorios. New forms of literature appeared: the novel (Defoe's *Robinson Crusoe*, Richardson's *Pamela*, and Fielding's *Tom Jones*), biography of a new type (Boswell's *Life of Samuel Johnson*), popular history (Hume's *History of England* and Gibbon's *Decline and Fall of the Roman Empire*), and the periodical essay (those of Addison and Steele in *The Tatler* and *The Spectator*). The first daily newspapers were established in London, and the first monthly magazine appeared.

The British Empire was extended by the acquisition of Canada, Gibraltar, Malta, and Ceylon. Robert Clive and Warren Hastings achieved supremacy in India for the British. Captain James Cook explored the Pacific from Australia and New Zealand to California and Hawaii for more than a decade. George Vancouver explored the northwest coast of America. James Bruce penetrated Africa in a daring expedition and found the source of the Blue Nile. Commercial and naval supremacy were won from the Dutch early in the century, and London replaced Amsterdam as the foremost center of shipping and finance in Europe.

Technological changes were building the foundations of industrialism. The cotton textile industry was transformed by a series of innovations that created the modern form of cloth manufacture, ushered in the Industrial Revolution, and made Lancashire and Liverpool great manufacturing and shipping centers. In 1738 John Kay invented a "flying shuttle" which greatly speeded up weaving and created a shortage of yarn. This led to the development of a spinning machine in the mid-1760's by James Hargreaves, an illiterate weaver and carpenter. An improved spinning machine developed by Richard Arkwright, a former barber, appeared a few years later. By 1779 Samuel Crompton, son of a small farmer, had perfected a spinning "mule" that could produce the finest yarn in much larger quantities than before; Crompton's invention was stolen and he died in poverty, but he gave the English cotton textile industry its greatest stimulus. The ability to produce yarn in greater amounts vastly increased the demand for cotton, and in America Eli Whitney developed the cotton gin, which mechanically cleaned the cotton boll. The growing of cotton throughout the world was greatly expanded, as was the plantation slavery system in America.

Industrial innovations had been preceded by the development of new machinery and methods in agriculture. Jethro Tull, a gentleman farmer, early in the eighteenth century developed a drill for planting seeds and introduced the practice of planting in rows. Charles Townshend, grandfather of Adam Smith's benefactor and a prominent statesman, retired from political life in 1730 to devote his time to the development of new crops, especially fodder crops such as turnips and clover. This was an important breakthrough: formerly land had to remain fallow to recoup its fertility, but now it could grow animal feed crops and still be "rested" for a year. Robert Bakewell, another successful farmer, developed techniques of stock breeding and introduced improved methods of livestock management. Arthur Young, the great writer on agriculture, spent most of his life publicizing the new methods and advocating enclosures as necessary to their adoption. The new agricultural techniques required larger farms, increased capital, and fenced-in fields, and from 1760 to 1830 the open lands of England were extensively fenced and hedged. Small farms and the village common disappeared in favor of larger acreage. Increased agricultural output and lower costs of production meant that greater numbers of the population could join the labor force in the growing industrial cities.

These were only a few of the leading events and the major personalities associated with them. Thousands of other people in commerce and industry, agriculture, exploration and empire building, the arts, and other aspects of English life took advantage of opportunities with initiative and imagination. Many were of humble origin. Even in politics, the last stronghold of privilege, a few new men like Edmund Burke were able to work up to positions of prominence and power.

This was the practical, everyday side of the social process that philosophers like Smith tried to analyze. They could see all around them an economy in ferment, with change the order of the day. Progress was being made because of the individual efforts of thousands of people acting for themselves alone. There seemed to be no order or reason behind the process, yet mankind was certainly moving onward — perhaps haltingly, but nevertheless onward — to what appeared to be a better world. In one respect there was a theoretical problem to solve — what were the principles that produced orderly social relationships in an individualistic, competitive, changing society? In another respect the problem was quite practical — would government regulation and control impede or advance the progress of such a society?

THE SOLUTION: ECONOMIC FREEDOM

Adam Smith advocated a "system of natural liberty," in which each individual would be left free to pursue and advance his own interests. This system, he argued, would result in the greatest wealth both for the individual and for society. Indeed, the very effort of the individual to serve himself would bring maximum benefits for society as a whole and for other individuals. This was the simple underlying principle that would enable social order to develop in an individualistic society.

The advocates of mercantilism and government regulation had assumed that the selfish desires of individuals would lead to less wealth for all unless human actions were regulated and controlled. More for me means less for you, was the assumption, unless men's efforts were directed toward more for all.

This argument was wrong, said Smith. If I want something from you, I must produce something you want and exchange it for what you have. Both of us benefit, because we both give up something that has less value to us than does the product we receive in exchange; hence the welfare of both is increased over what it would otherwise be. As Smith phrased it:

> It is not from the benevolence of the butcher, the brewer, or the baker, that we expect our dinner, but from their regard to their own interest. We address ourselves, not to their humanity but to their self-love, and never talk to them of our own necessities but of their advantages.

According to Smith, self-interest in a free society would also lead to the most rapid progress and growth a nation was capable of achieving. People would save in order to improve their own positions and in so doing would add more capital to the nation's resources. They would use that capital in the most profitable way and in so doing produce the things that others wanted most. Even where laws and regulations impeded the businessman's freedom to invest where he wished, these motives would be so strong that they would still lead to growth and wealth:

> The uniform, constant, and uninterrupted effort of every man to better his condition, the principle from which public and national, as well as private opulence is originally derived, is frequently powerful enough to maintain the natural progress of things toward improvement, in spite both of the extravagance of government, and of the greatest errors of administration.

The greatest hindrance to economic progress was government, in Adam Smith's view. In the system of natural liberty there were only three legitimate functions of government: the establishment and maintenance of justice, national defense, and "erecting and maintaining certain public works and certain public institutions, which it can never be for the interest of any individual, or small number of individuals, to erect and maintain." Smith did not admit much into this last category, however. Roads and communications, yes—but their cost should be borne by the user through tolls rather than by the general taxpayer. Education and religious instruction, maybe—they were of general benefit but could be provided by private enterprise or voluntary contributions as well as by government. Any other government undertaking would be more harmful than beneficial, even though the best of motives were behind it:

> Every system which endeavors . . . to draw towards a particular species of industry a greater share of the capital of the society than what would naturally go to it . . . retards, instead of accelerating, the progress of the society towards real wealth and greatness.

Although Smith definitely looked with disfavor upon government enterprise, it should not be supposed that he would give business a completely free hand. He was aware of the tendency of businessmen to conspire to their own advantage against the public:

> People of the same trade seldom meet together, even for merriment and diversion, but the conversation ends in a conspiracy against the public, or in some contrivance to raise prices.

Nevertheless, Smith was not afraid of monopoly. He lived in a simpler age than ours, before the growth of great enterprises and giant industrial plants. The only example of industrial production in his book is a pin factory in which some two dozen handicraft workers were employed. In those days the capital required for entry into almost any trade was small, technology was simple and available to all, and monopoly existed only where special privileges were granted and protected by government. Smith was confident that no private monopoly unprotected by government could long endure: monopoly profits would immediately invite competition, which would destroy the monopoly.

THE SELF-ADJUSTING MARKET

If self-interest was the driving force of the economy, the mechanism through which it worked was a system of self-adjusting markets. Competition among sellers in an effort to make profits would naturally result in a pattern of production fitted to the needs and desires of consumers, while profits would be held to a minimum amount just large enough to motivate producers.

Every commodity, according to Smith, has a "natural" price. In primitive societies it is determined by the amount of labor needed for production. In more advanced societies, those in which private property has developed, the natural price depends on costs of production—the amount that must be paid for wages, rent, and profit. Whenever the market price of a commodity differs from its natural price, market forces are set in motion to move it back. As Smith explains it:

> When the price of any commodity is neither more nor less than what is sufficient to pay the rent of the land, the wages of the labour, and the profits of the stock employed in raising, preparing, and bringing it to market, according to their natural rates, the commodity is then sold for what may be called its natural price . . . precisely for what it is worth, or for what it really costs the person who brings it to market. . . .
>
> When the quantity of any commodity which is brought to market falls short of the effectual demand, all those who are willing to pay . . . cannot be supplied with the quantity which they want. . . . Some of them will be willing to give more. A competition will immediately begin among them, and the market price will rise. . . .
>
> When the quantity brought to market exceeds the effectual demand, it cannot be all sold to those who are willing to pay the whole value of the rent, wages and profit, which must be paid in order to bring it thither. . . . The market price will sink. . . .

These changes in price set in motion corresponding changes in
the amount produced. When the market price of a commodity is
greater than its natural price, more of that commodity will be produced and brought to market. On the other hand, production will fall
when the market price is below the natural price and when, therefore,
the resources used in production cannot be paid at their natural rates.
Again, Smith describes how production responds to price relationships:

supply + demand

> The quantity of every commodity brought to market natu-
> rally suits itself to the effectual demand. . . . If at any time it
> exceeds the effectual demand, some of the component parts of its
> price must be paid below their natural rate. If it is rent, the inter-
> est of the landlords will immediately prompt them to withdraw a
> part of their land; and if it is wages or profit, the interest of the
> labourers in the one case, and of their employers in the other, will
> prompt them to withdraw a part of their labour or stock from this
> employment. The quantity brought to market will soon be no
> more than sufficient to supply the effectual demand. All the dif-
> ferent parts of its price will rise to their natural rate, and the
> whole price to its natural price.
>
> If on the contrary, the quantity brought to market should at
> any time fall short of the effectual demand, some of the component
> parts of its price must rise above their natural rate. If it is rent,
> the interest of all other landlords will naturally prompt them to
> prepare more land for the raising of this commodity; if it is wages
> or profit, the interest of all other labourers and dealers will soon
> prompt them to employ more labour and stock in preparing and
> bringing it to market. The quantity brought thither will soon be
> sufficient to supply the effectual demand. All the different parts of
> its price will soon sink to their natural rate, and its whole price to
> its natural price.
>
> The natural price, therefore, is, as it were, the central price, to
> which the prices of all commodities are continually gravitating.
> Different accidents may sometimes keep them suspended a good
> deal above it, and sometimes force them down even somewhat
> below it. But whatever may be the obstacles which hinder them
> from settling in this center of repose and continuance, they are
> constantly tending towards it.
>
> The whole quantity of industry annually employed in order to
> bring any commodity to market, naturally suits itself in this man-
> ner to the effectual demand. It naturally aims at bringing always
> that precise quantity thither which may be sufficient to supply,
> and no more than supply, that demand.

Turkey, in Indostan, and I believe, in most other govern-
of Asia.

was well aware that economic growth brings change and
As capital is accumulated the natural progress of opulence
from agriculture to manufacturing to commerce, and the
ciety exhibits prosperity in all three areas. A developing
gives rise to the growth of towns, which in turn offer a
rket for agricultural products, and a developed urban and
ety offers widened opportunities for trade and shipping.
trade further stimulates manufacturing and specialized
al production for export. Population increases as productiv-
acilitating still broader market expansion and stimulating still
cialization and capital accumulation.

his process the economy moves forward to higher and higher
development, raising the whole social order with it. Yet it
ously maintains the orderly market equilibrium that con-
tends toward a pattern of production fitted to effectual
The system of natural liberty produces an equilibrium of
oving always toward opulence.

SMITH'S ACHIEVEMENT

m Smith's analysis of the market economy emphasized that
alism resulted in order, not chaos. Even though each person
d with all others for wealth and profit, their very competition
d market forces that led to an orderly increase in the wealth
ation. The desire for prosperity, coupled with a natural tend-
trade and exchange, led to specialization, investment of capi-
stable economic growth. The free economy served the indi-
whose needs and desires were met by the natural tendency of
rs to make and sell what consumers desired. The welfare of
munity was thereby maximized.

e moral dilemma of earlier writers was resolved by Smith's
, in that there was no conflict between individual and social
s. The whole structure rested on the free, competitive play of
al selfishness. The motives lauded by Mandeville a half-
y earlier were shown by Smith to be the source of economic
, social order, and general welfare. The path to brotherhood—at
economic affairs—lay through competitive selfishness. Adam
had thus provided social philosophers and moralists with answers
blems that had gone unresolved for a century.

addition, Smith presented future economists with the analytical
work of the science of economics. His vision of a competitive
t equilibrium following a path of growth to affluence and abun-

Little has been added in the last two centuries to this description
of market equilibrium. Contemporary economists use the term *normal*
rather than *natural* price, and they are more careful to spell out the
exact conditions under which it prevails. A much more complex
analysis of production costs has been developed, and the process by
which the level of output responds to price has been analyzed in even
greater detail. But the basic descriptions of how supply and demand
determine an equilibrium price, of how competition pushes that price
to a level that just covers production costs, and of how production
responds to demand have remained fundamentally unchanged in the
writings of successive generations of economists.

Smith's analysis of the self-adjusting market economy had tremendous significance. It showed that production will automatically
adjust to the pattern of consumer demand, whatever that demand
may be and however it may shift and change. It showed that competition among sellers will drive prices down to the lowest possible level
consistent with continued production at levels satisfactory to consumers. It showed that resources will be used in the most efficient and
economical manner—using as the criterion of efficiency and economy
the satisfaction of consumer wants at the lowest possible prices consistent with continued production at the desired levels. And it showed
that all this could be accomplished through the free operation of
market forces, with no interference or direction from government or
any other agency of economic management.

Smith emphasized, however, that these ideal results could be
precluded by abridgements of full freedom in economic activity, such
as "secrets in manufactures," "secrets in trade," "singularity of soil and
situation," "monopoly," and "all those laws which restrain . . . competition." Smith was particularly opposed to monopoly in all of its
forms, and some of his most pungent comments point to its evils:

> The monopolists, by keeping the market continually under-
> stocked, by never fully supplying the effectual demand, sell their
> commodities much above the natural price, and raise their emolu-
> ments, whether they consist in wages or profit, greatly above their
> natural rate.
> The price of monopoly . . . is upon every occasion the
> highest which can be squeezed out of the buyers. . . .

Whatever the source of the restrictions on economic freedom that led
to monopoly—whether government, business, or labor—Adam Smith
was opposed to it.

TWO QUALIFICATIONS

At this point it is important to note two limitations on Smith's
analysis of the free market. These limitations were at the heart of

criticisms developed by socialists of the nineteenth century, and theories of later economists have not satisfactorily overcome them.

The first limitation concerns the nature of "effectual demand" and its dependence on the pattern of income distribution. It is fine to argue that production will match itself to the pattern of consumer demand, but if the distribution of income is highly unequal, that pattern will provide much to the rich and little to the poor. Unless the distribution of income is right and proper, it does little good to argue that production is efficient and economical. If the distribution of income is wrong, the pattern of production will be wrong also, no matter how efficiently the free market works to match production with demand. This basic problem was almost immediately raised by the socialists spawned by the early Industrial Revolution, and it was shortly thereafter expanded by Karl Marx into a theory of the breakdown of capitalism. Later generations of economists have attempted to provide answers to the problem—most successfully in the 1890–1910 period—with results that have not been fully satisfactory.

The second limitation, closely related to that of economic justice, concerns private property in land and capital. Adam Smith, as a good economic liberal, supported the institution of private property as both natural and necessary to the preservation of economic incentives. However, he granted its necessity only in advanced societies. In primitive society, only labor needed a reward as a factor of production, and the cost of production consisted of wages alone; but in advanced societies, rent on land and profit on capital became part of the costs of production. This qualification spoiled Smith's grand scheme of an equilibrium of *natural* forces in the market. In the case of rent and profit the costs of production were clearly the products of social organization, not natural phenomena in the same sense as human labor and the motive of self-interest.

Socialists were quick to seize upon these gaps in Smith's logic. Only a return to labor was natural, they argued, and only when the full value of output was gained by labor through social ownership of land and capital would the natural state of society be recaptured. Then economic justice could also be achieved, for the entire product of society would go to those who worked and the pattern of effectual demand would not be distorted by unearned income. In later chapters the dialogue on economic justice between the critics and the supporters of the existing order will be explored in greater detail.

ECONOMIC GROWTH

Adam Smith was not primarily concerned with these matters of justice in income distribution, and they did not become topics of major concern to economists until after the rise of socialism. Smith was far

more concerned with economic growth society to higher levels, which he also e motives inherent in the psychology of the ral and inevitable in a free society.

The "progress of opulence," accord result of three factors: division of labor, w mulation of capital. As productivity rises ments, "a general plenty diffuses itself thr of the society."

Specialization in production and divis inherent human "propensity to truck, bart for another," according to Smith. Only n "nobody ever saw a dog make a fair and d bone for another with another dog." More cal inclination that leads men to trade, and ization, also makes men dependent upon engenders the complex social fabric of the m old-fashioned view, however: the modern people specialize in producing one thing produce everything they need because their are thereby increased.

Just as exchange gives rise to specializati Smith said, "the extent of this division must a the extent of the market." When the marke devote himself to producing only one produc expands, he can specialize and thereby gain creased efficiency. Wider markets lead to great productivity, and greater wealth, and to the use overcome the difficulties of barter in a system relationships.

None of this economic growth can occur wit capital, gathered out of savings and used to fu tivity and promote still greater specialization and Accumulation of capital was seen as the key to But the whole process depended on security of

In all countries where there is tolerable s common understanding will endeavor to em he can command, in procuring either prese ture profit. . . . A man must be perfectly cra is tolerable security, does not employ all the s mands, whether it be his own or borrowed of

In those unfortunate countries, indeed, w tinually afraid of the violence of their superio bury and conceal a great part of their stock . .

dance defined the problems that the science of economics has wrestled with ever since. His formulation of the solutions — the self-adjusting market and the process of capital accumulation — was the starting point for a complex theoretical system that later economists have richly elaborated. Smith's purely scientific contribution has been vast, and in its basic structure his framework still remains the heart of scientific economics.

It is easy to see why the *Wealth of Nations* is one of the great books of Western civilization. At one level, it is a polemic written for its own time and directed against the existing practices and policies of government. At another, it is a philosophical treatise that deals with fundamental problems of order and chaos in human society. Finally, it is a scientific treatise that analyzes the principles on which the economic system functions. All three themes are so closely intertwined that no one aspect of the argument stands alone, but each supports the others. It is a fascinating amalgam of ideology, philosophy, and scientific analysis.

Chapter

4

Classical Economics

Adam Smith founded a "school" of economics. Particularly strong in England, Smith's followers dominated the field in both Europe and the United States for almost a century. They represented the orthodox approach to economic problems and policy up to the last quarter of the nineteenth century and were united by their acceptance of Smith's liberalism and his system of natural liberty. Their analytical system was based on Smith's equilibrium of supply, demand, and competitive markets, and they generally favored freedom of action for business enterprise and strong limitations on government. They were internationalists and stood for free trade and free movement of capital. "Classical economics" is the name usually given to this style of thinking.

Four other economists besides Smith made major contributions to the classical system. These men were Thomas R. Malthus, David Ricardo, Jeremy Bentham, and Jean Baptiste Say. Working primarily in the turbulent first quarter of the nineteenth century, when the world economy was percolating with the changes wrought by war, revolution, economic change, population growth, new technologies, and political upheaval, they sought to analyze the economy in terms of a few basic underlying principles. In doing so, they turned economics into the first social "science."

ENGLAND'S REACTION TO THE FRENCH REVOLUTION

Adam Smith's *Wealth of Nations* had just been published when an age of revolution began — the great political and social revolutions in the American colonies and later in France that wiped away the last vestige of European feudalism and the old aristocratic order. There was a good deal of sympathy in England for the American revolutionists, since many Englishmen felt that their own society retained unwanted remnants of the old order. One of the reasons for the success of the American Revolution was undoubtedly the opposition of English liberals to continuing the war. Political reform was a particularly strong issue in England since many members of Parliament represented districts with very small populations, while some large cities, emerging as a result of the Industrial Revolution, had no representation whatsoever.

Many Englishmen looked with favor upon the French Revolution, too. They thought it would bring democracy to France, develop a society similar to that of England, and establish peace between two nations that had been at war intermittently for more than a hundred years. Charles James Fox, leader of the liberal Whig party, praised the fall of the Bastille, calling it the "greatest event . . . that ever happened in the world." Even William Pitt, the Tory prime minister, felt that the Revolution would enable France to become more like England, and he forecast fifteen years of peace and tranquility between the two nations.

There were, of course, conservatives who took a stand against the French Revolution from the very beginning. Edmund Burke, for example, in his *Reflections on the French Revolution* (1790), opposed the treatment of the French king and aristocrats by the French mob and feared that freedom, justice, and order would be destroyed by the growing radicalism of the "swinish multitudes."[1] When the Reign of Terror began, British opinion shifted to support the conservative position. The intellectual leaders who favored the Revolution — such as Thomas Paine, who wrote *The Rights of Man* in 1790 as an answer to Burke — were discredited. Some changed their minds to support the conservative position. Prime Minister William Pitt had come into office on a platform of social and economic reform but turned to a policy of uncompromising conservatism. At one point he stated, "Seeing that where the greatest changes have taken place, the most dreadful con-

[1]The title of this book is taken from a passage in Burke's *Reflections:* "The age of chivalry is dead, that of sophisters, oeconomists and calculators has succeeded, and the glory of Europe is extinguished forever." Even in those days the economist was considered to be a liberal reformer.

sequences have ensued . . . and . . . seeing that in this general shock the constitution of Great Britain has remained pure and unchanged in its vital principles . . . I think it right to declare my most decided opinion, that . . . even the slightest change in such a constitution must be considered an evil." The policy of the British government became one of maintaining the status quo, resisting reform, and — worse — suppressing liberal points of view.

When the wars with France began, legal action was taken in England to "prevent disloyalty." In 1795 the Habeas Corpus Act was suspended for five years; all secret associations were banned; all lecture rooms where admission was charged were legally classified as brothels, in order to prevent meetings; any meeting attended by more than fifty persons had to be superintended by a magistrate; all printing presses had to be registered with the government; export of English newspapers was prohibited; the Corresponding Society, a group of liberals who tried to spread news of liberal causes by writing letters, was suppressed in 1799. In that year and the next the Anti-Combination Laws were passed, which prohibited any kind of combination of either workers or employers for the purpose of regulating conditions of employment. There is no record that the laws were enforced against employers, but workmen were prosecuted and nascent labor unions destroyed. An atmosphere of suppression prevailed.

Although reform was prevented, the march of events could not be halted. The war years of the late eighteenth and early nineteenth centuries were years of broad and rapid change. Industrialization was greatly stimulated by wartime demands. The agricultural revolution was speeded up by wartime increases in the price of food. Population was growing rapidly and shifting from rural to urban. As cities grew, slums, inadequate sewage and water systems, and all the other urban ills developed on a large scale. The multitude of economic and social problems generated by these vast changes went unsolved, while "the Establishment" concerned itself with holding the line and rooting out the "radicals."

MALTHUS AND THE THEORY OF POPULATION

One of the most pressing problems that emerged during the years of the French wars concerned the poor. They had always been present in England, but in the former aristocratic, rural society, each parish had traditionally cared for its own. A tax on landowners was expected to provide relief funds for those who could not support themselves, while the parish was supposed to find work for the able-bodied poor. A philosophy of *noblesse oblige* prevailed.

This ancient system broke down, however. Wartime increases in food prices, the agricultural revolution and the enclosures of common land which displaced many farmers from their small plots, the Industrial Revolution, and growing cities and population brought on serious problems of poverty. Displaced farmers might have found work in handicraft manufacture of cloth, which had long been a rural occupation, but industrialization had destroyed that opportunity; indeed, a whole generation of rural cottagers lost their livelihood with the rise of textile mills in the growing cities. Growth of the armed forces offered a way out for some of the able-bodied young men, but it was not a general solution.

The conservative reaction engendered by the French Revolution meant that new measures to alleviate poverty were politically impossible. Anything smacking in the least degree of reform was anathema to English policy-makers. Yet the great increase in the number of poor people put a tremendous financial burden on the wealthier landowners. Something had to give.

The solution was provided by an obscure young minister named Thomas Robert Malthus (1766-1834). Like all good conservatives in a time when serious problems abound, he found the cause of the crisis not in any recent developments or changes that might be amended by policy actions but in large forces over which governments have little or no control. The problem of the poor was essentially moral, he argued, and had its origins in two fundamental propositions. First, "food is necessary to the existence of man." Second, "the passion between the sexes is necessary and will remain nearly in its present state." These two facts led to the principle that "the power of population is infinitely greater than the power in the earth to produce subsistence for man."

In other words, population would tend to increase unless it was held in check by "misery and vice." If the supply of food were to increase, there would be a corresponding increase in population until the amount of food per person had fallen back to the subsistence level, at which point the increase in population would stop. Wages would always tend toward the subsistence level. Any increase in wages above that level would only cause the working population to grow and wages to fall back once more to subsistence. Conversely, if the price of food rose, wage rates would likewise be forced upward to maintain a subsistence level. One way or another, there was a natural rate of wages which always tended toward the level of subsistence.

Consider the implications of this doctrine. Paying relief would not solve the problem of poverty but would merely increase the income of the poor and enable them to raise more children. Poverty would continue because there would be no increase in food supplies for the larger population. It was not necessary, therefore, to look to economic or social causes to explain the problems of the poor. They were caused by the old system of poor relief, which had continuously generated more poverty until the crisis had finally come. The solution was obviously to eliminate the relief system.

Assistance to the poor worsened the situation in another way. By increasing the numbers of the poor, the relief system shifted wealth from those who used it productively to an idle poverty-stricken population. Wealth that should have been invested to provide jobs was wasted on maintaining the poor in idleness, and the whole economic growth of the nation was slowed down.

The Malthusian view had other important implications. The causes of poverty were not rooted in the structure of society, in the distribution of income, in inequalities in the ownership of wealth, or in any of the many institutions of society. Neither the wealthy nor society as a whole was at fault. The poor were responsible for their own fate. All they had to do to eliminate their poverty was to have fewer children.

Even the formation of labor unions was useless, according to Malthus. Higher wages would result only in a larger population and a rise in the cost of food as more people used the wage increases to bid up food prices. The end result would be a shift of wealth from businessmen through the hands of workers into the pockets of unproductive landowners. The amount of capital available for economic expansion would be reduced just as population increased, leaving the nation worse off in the long run. Furthermore, unions meant strikes, and strikes meant reduced output, lower profits, and less capital accumulation. No, labor unions were not a solution.

Malthus' principle of population was indeed a dismal theorem —for the poor. But it was a great doctrine for conservatives, because it gave them the best of reasons for doing nothing about a serious problem. Malthus himself, an educated, religious gentleman, felt compassion and pity for the poor. He expressed it many times, and there is no reason to doubt his sincerity. But his analysis told him that social action would only hinder instead of help. The only permanent solution was moral reform of the individual.

The Malthusian principle of population was to become one of the major building blocks of classical economics, and it remained the basis of wage theories for a century. Despite its essentially pessimistic point of view, however, it did provide one avenue of hope for economic growth. Economic expansion could provide increased food supplies which would cause increases in the labor force necessary to achieve further economic growth. Malthus showed that the size of the labor force was not a barrier to economic expansion. Manpower resources would emerge as the economy grew. All that was needed was capital to get the process started.

Malthus also helped later economists clarify one of the key relationships necessary for betterment of the human condition. Production had to increase faster than population if there was to be any major improvement in living standards. Europe and North America, in the ensuing era of industrialization, succeeded in achieving that relationship and are vastly better off today than they were in Malthus' time. Many other countries, in which population growth exceeds expansion of production, have millions of people who are doomed to the "misery and vice" of the Malthusian analysis.

RICARDO AND ECONOMIC GROWTH

David Ricardo (1772-1823) was the apostle of capital accumulation. In his view, the growth of capital was the great source of economic expansion, and all economic policy should be directed toward promoting it. To prove his point he developed a theoretical model of the economy that dominated the thinking of economists for fifty years. He believed that economic freedom led to maximum profits, that profits were the source of investment capital, and that a competitive economy would lead to profit-maximizing investments. In Ricardo's view, policies that benefited business would lead to maximum economic growth.

Born in London of Jewish parents, Ricardo married a Quaker girl when he reached the age of twenty-one, causing a break between himself and his stockbroker father. Financed by friends, he became a trader on the London Exchange. So adept was he at the intricate and risky business of speculation that by the age of twenty-six he had amassed a large fortune. He retired to a country estate in 1814, bought an Irish pocket-borough seat in Parliament in 1819, and devoted the rest of his life to public affairs and economics. A "millionaire radical," he advocated reforms in banking and currency, poor relief, the tariff, and freedom of press and speech, and he supported other reform causes. His only book on economics carries the formidable title *Principles of Political Economy and Taxation.* Its content is even more formidable, but it had tremendous influence in its day.

In the years around 1815, at the close of the Napoleonic wars, one of the great political and social issues in England was whether the nation should try to preserve its agriculturally-based economy or become more heavily industrialized. Involved in the debate was the whole question of the place of the landed aristocracy in the English social and political system. The issue was fought out in Parliament over the Corn Laws, which dealt with the import of grain into England. (Englishmen call grain "corn," and corn is "Indian corn.") English laws related to the import of wheat were intended to promote domestic agriculture without causing major increases in the price of food. When the price of wheat fell in England, tariffs were raised on imports of wheat in order to keep out the foreign grain that was depressing domestic prices and injuring the business of domestic farmers; when the price of wheat rose above a given level, import duties were reduced, thus encouraging more imports and keeping domestic prices from rising further. In short, the British government tried to keep grain prices between an upper and a lower limit by means of a sliding scale of tariffs.

Nevertheless, during the French wars the price of food rose substantially and farmers were well off. Their production costs also rose and remained high when peace came, wartime demand slackened, and the price of food fell. Farmers began clamoring for higher duties on imported wheat, fearing that they faced ruin unless protected by enforcement of the Corn Laws. The landowner's point of view was reinforced by arguments that a sound agriculture was necessary for England's national defense and for the preservation of the old traditions and national vigor. There was a revival of the physiocratic doctrine that economic growth depended on the natural productivity of the soil. Pamphlets appeared, such as one entitled "England Independent of Commerce," which argued for the protection and preservation of agricultural interests.

Business interests, on the other hand, opposed tariff increases, which, they declared, would raise food prices and force wages upward. The result would be reduced profits, decreased exports of manufactured products, and ruin for English industry. Businessmen believed that England's future lay with industrial expansion, not with agriculture, and they demanded outright repeal of the Corn Laws.

This was the state of the issue when Ricardo and other economists entered the debate over Corn Law policy. Ricardo was on the businessman's side of the argument. He believed that landowners, not farmers, would be the chief beneficiaries if the price of wheat in England was raised by a higher tariff. The high price of wheat would enable cultivation to be extended to areas that would otherwise be unprofitable. In older wheat-growing areas, rents would be raised to take advantage of the higher prices farmers were receiving. A larger proportion of the total national income would then flow into the hands of landowners, and this parasitic group would use its increased wealth for luxury expenditures such as servants and country houses, not for productive investment.

In addition, the enlarged cultivation of land would draw capital and labor away from industry and distort the whole production pattern of the country. Artificially high food prices would lead to a misallocation of productive resources into agriculture and out of manufacturing, thereby hindering the nation's natural development of industry.

Ricardo also pointed out that high prices for food would require high wage rates and high costs of production in manufacturing. Since England had to sell her manufactures throughout the world, competing with the products of other countries, higher costs in English industry would result in reduced business for English exports and a reduced level of output for English manufacturers. Profits would also be reduced, and there would be a slower pace of capital accumulation and economic expansion, due to the lack of both incentive and funds to invest.

This was Ricardo's indictment of the Corn Laws (although he did not advocate their complete repeal). It supported the businessman's position on the issue with a theoretical model of the economy that gave substance and validity to his policy conclusions. Ricardo's theory was more than a treatment of a contemporary policy problem. If that were all it had been, it would have died as interest in the problem died. But Ricardo took it much further and generalized it into a comprehensive theory of economic growth.

In the early stages of a nation's growth the population would be small and only a portion of the land would be cultivated. Under these conditions the rent paid to landowners would be a relatively small proportion, and profits a large proportion, of the total national income. The profits, plowed back into industrial development, would result in a greater demand for labor, which—following Malthus— would cause population to grow while wages remained at the subsistence level. The growth in population would require an extension of the cultivated area in order to provide larger amounts of food. This extension could be accomplished only by raising food prices to cover the higher costs of production incurred by bringing less fertile lands into cultivation. The higher price of food would enable landowners to raise the rents charged on the older cultivated lands, because the higher food prices charged could bear higher rents. At the same time, the higher cost of food would force employers to pay higher *money* wages in order to maintain wage rates at the subsistence level. This in turn would raise the cost of manufactured goods and thereby reduce the profits obtained by businessmen. The reduced profits would then leave less wealth available for expansion and would also reduce incentives to invest. Ricardo envisaged that this process of economic growth would continue, with capital accumulation and growth gradually slowing down until, after many decades of expansion, growth halted. At this stage of development the population would be large, cultivation extended, industry developed, production high—but savings and capital accumulation would be adequate only for replacement of capital, not further expansion.

The picture Ricardo drew was one in which the economy, if left alone, would achieve the maximum growth possible. To that end, businessmen would have to be freed of all restrictions that might reduce their ability to maximize profits, so that the maximum amount of saving and capital accumulation could take place. Government intervention in the economy would lead to a lower rather than a higher level of economic activity. Right or wrong, the theory was on the side of the coming rulers of the social order—business interests— and this in itself ensured it long life.

THE INTERNATIONAL ECONOMY

One of the strengths of Ricardian economics was its applicability to the international economy. For the first time, an analysis of the domestic economy based on the fundamentals of land, labor, and capital could be applied rigorously to international economic relationships. This represented a major step forward in the development of economics as a science. One of the goals of all scientific endeavor is the building of broader and broader generalizations that encompass an ever-widening body of phenomena. Science advances by stripping away details and constructing general laws, and Ricardian economics did this by reducing all economic phenomena to fundamental relationships between the factors of production.

The integration of the international economy into the Ricardian model was done in two ways. First, Ricardo showed that international specialization and division of labor was advantageous to all nations and that restrictive trade policies designed to protect domestic producers would injure the nation that imposed them. Free trade was the road to economic well-being internationally as well as domestically. The argument for this position, embodied in the famous law of comparative advantage, is complex, but Ricardo was able to prove its validity. He showed that as long as it costs less to produce cloth in England than it does to produce wheat, *compared with costs in other countries*, it will pay Englishmen to shift their resources to cloth manufactures, export the product, and import wheat from other countries.

For example, suppose it takes Englishmen one day's labor to produce a yard of cloth and two days' labor to grow a bushel of wheat; then wheat costs twice as much effort as cloth. Suppose also that it takes Frenchmen one day's labor to produce each product. In this case, Englishmen should produce cloth (one day's labor), export it to France, trade it one-for-one for wheat, and import the wheat back to England. In this way Englishmen would get, for one day's labor, the wheat it would otherwise take them two days to produce. The Frenchmen would also benefit. They could produce wheat, ship it to England and trade one bushel for *two* yards of cloth, and ship the cloth back to France. They would also receive products worth two days' effort for one day's actual work. Both sides would benefit from this specialization and free exchange.

But the process would not end there. The export of English cloth to France would drive its selling price down, and increased domestic production would push costs of production up. The same would happen for French wheat. As these price changes took place, the growing import-export trade between the two countries would establish an equilibrium of prices and trade. England would both produce and export much cloth, but its output of wheat would be small and most of its supplies would be imported. The opposite would be true of France. The two commodities would sell for equivalent prices in the two countries, for if they did not, further shifts in production, trade, prices, and costs would occur. In this way an international equilibrium would be established in which the world pattern of production would be optimized.

This analysis of international economic equilibrium was supplemented by a second approach, this time in the field of economic development. The preceding section of this chapter described the Ricardian theory of the stationary economy, in which the return to capital was so low that only replacement of worn-out capital equipment occurred. As the return to capital in one country fell, however, profit-maximizing investors would seek higher returns by investing in less well-developed countries abroad. Capital exports from the mature economies would flow quickly to the newly developing countries, and they in turn would be brought to higher levels of production and wealth. Of course, they would have to offer political stability and protection to private property, but aside from that qualification the classical economist could look forward to a whole world moving gradually toward opulence.

In this way Ricardo and his followers applied Adam Smith's concepts of orderly growth and market equilibrium to the international economic system. Only national rivalry, with its tariffs, trade restrictions, and wars, could interfere with the developmental process. It is perhaps ironic that the part of his theory which Ricardo thought most important—the theory of economic growth—has been largely discarded by modern economists, although they retain his stress on capital accumulation. But the theory of international economic equilibrium, which was only a minor part of the original analysis, remains an integral part of modern economics in almost its original form.

SAY'S LAW OF MARKETS

Only one major element had to be added to classical economics to complete its systematic analysis of the economy: an examination of production and employment levels. It had been shown that a free market would allocate resources so that production would adjust to consumer needs and wants, that output would grow through savings and capital accumulation, that income would be distributed among social classes according to natural laws, and that the same principles applied to both domestic and international economic relationships. Still to be determined was whether a free market would also maintain full employment of men and capital.

The issue was not merely academic. The Industrial Revolution had brought economic instability, aggravated in the early years of the nineteenth century by the on-again, off-again wars against Napoleon. When peace came in 1815 the economic stimulus of government spending was withdrawn from the economies of both England and the Continent. Demand for industrial products fell from its wartime levels, and England was faced with competition from the Continent for the worldwide markets she had kept largely to herself. Soldiers and sailors returning to the civilian economy and handicraft workers displaced by factory production increased the number of workers seeking employment. These problems were compounded in England by the fact that industrialization had proceeded farthest there.

England's economic situation was further aggravated by government monetary policies that resulted in "tight" money and a shortage of credit just when the economy needed a stimulus. During the war years prices had risen substantially, credit had been much expanded, and the Bank of England had stopped redeeming its paper currency in gold. Increases in the national debt had been one of the major causes of the credit expansion and the price increases. Economists, led by Ricardo, blamed the inflation on excessive issuance of paper money and prescribed when the war ended that the Bank of England again redeem paper currency in gold at the levels that had prevailed before the war, even though there was not enough gold to sustain the existing amounts of currency and credit then outstanding. The economy was to be given a dose of deflation.

This early application of principles of sound finance was based on an incorrect diagnosis of the economic illness, and the remedy turned out to be worse than the disease. Inflation had been largely due to expansion of total spending during the war years, promoted in part by increases in the money supply, at a time when output could be increased only slowly. Prices had to rise, and the amount of currency and credit reflected this expansion of a relatively fully employed economy. By prescribing deflation as the cure for inflation, economists were able to bring prices down, but only at the expense of output and employment. Like any deflation after inflation, creditors and owners of financial assets benefited — at the expense of unemployed workers and profitless businessmen. The burden of England's economic difficulties was shifted from owners of monetary assets to producers.

Hardship was widespread and business activity was in a generally depressed state for thirty years after 1815. The economy had its ups and downs during this period, and economic growth continued, but there was hardly a year in which England had full employment by modern standards. Several times, unemployment apparently rose to 40 or 50 per cent of the work force in the industrial cities of the midlands.

The instability of the economy had already aroused criticisms of industrialism and the new economic order. Even before 1815 Jean Simonde de Sismondi (1773–1842), a Frenchman traveling in England, had seen the industrial depressions and predicted that capital investment would periodically force the capacity to produce to outrun the ability to consume. His argument was echoed by an English physiocrat, William Spence (1783–1860), who pointed out in two pamphlets of 1807 and 1808 that capital investment in commerce and manufacturing created economic instability and insecurity, while the development of agriculture promoted economic stability and security. Spence called particular attention to the possibility that savings would reduce purchasing power and cause prosperity to disappear. Both Sismondi and Spence were disenchanted with industrialization, and each favored a different type of economic order—Spence the old aristocratic society and Sismondi a system that emphasized human and community values rather than individual gain. Their discussions of depressions were only part of more comprehensive attacks on the emerging business society.

Classical economists were quick to reply to these attacks. The basis of their rebuttal was a brief passage in a work by Jean Baptiste Say (1767–1832), a French popularizer of Adam Smith's work whose *A Treatise on Political Economy* had appeared in 1803. That work contained the first statement of the principle that came to be known as Say's Law of Markets, a concept that dominated the thinking of most economists on the level of economic activity until the Great Depression of the 1930's.

Say argued that there could never be a general deficiency of demand or a general glut of commodities throughout the whole economy. Certain industries or sectors of industry might be plagued by overproduction, due to miscalculation and excessive allocation of resources to those types of production, but elsewhere in the economy there would inevitably be shortages. The consequent fall of prices in one area and their rise in others would induce businessmen to shift production, and the imbalances would be quickly corrected.

People produce, he pointed out, not for the sake of producing but only to exchange their products for other goods they need and want. Since, therefore, production *is* demand, it is impossible for production in general to outrun demand. "Production creates its own demand" became the answer of the classical economists to the problem of business depressions.

In England, Say's argument was put forth by James Mill (1773–1836), father of the renowned philosopher and economist John Stuart

Mill, in an answer to Spence. The elder Mill wrote in 1807 that every increase in supply is an increase in demand—the more there is to sell, the more will be bought. The error in the theory of general glut, he maintained, is the confusion between a temporary dislocation in the process of exchange, which would be remedied by a new direction of industry, and the impossible case of an excess of wealth in general.

One economist remained unconvinced: Thomas R. Malthus. In his *Principles of Political Economy* (1820) Malthus devoted a long last chapter to developing a theory of economic stagnation based on inadequate "effectual demand." His argument, in brief, was that wages, being less than the total costs of production, cannot purchase the total output of industry, which causes prices to fall. The decline in prices reduces incentives to invest as well as profits that could be invested. The result is a general inadequacy of purchasing power that *could* continue indefinitely. A similar condition might result from excessive savings, which cause demand to fall, prices to decline, and stagnation to follow. The remedy, according to Malthus, was to reduce large incomes so that savings would not be excessive, to impose import tariffs and thereby promote a favorable balance of trade, and to spend for public works during bad times. A program of government intervention was needed because the free market economy could not regularly provide for full employment.

Malthus' argument was not developed with clarity and preciseness—he was not a rigorous theoretician—and his good friend David Ricardo made mincemeat of his theory of general glut in letters written to Malthus, in "Notes on Malthus' Principles of Political Economy" circulated among other economists, and in discussions at London's Political Economy Club. Since Ricardo's arguments *were* clear and precise, he carried the day.

Ricardo's answer to Malthus, in brief, recapitulated Say's Law of Markets in slightly more elaborate form. Savings are made not as an end in themselves but in order to employ labor in production. Mistakes can lead to a glut of a single commodity, but demand for all other commodities is not thereby reduced. A reallocation of productive effort will occur. Furthermore, unemployment causes wages to fall, inducing businessmen to hire the idle laborers with the capital created by savings. In this way, all capital is put back into use and all willing workers are once again employed. The basic cure, therefore, is not income redistribution and public works but lower wages and higher profits.

Ricardo's answer was supplemented by an extraordinarily perceptive volume originally published in 1802, Henry Thornton's *The Paper Credit of Great Britain*. This book had been written during the controversy over paper money, gold, and inflation, but its argument was adapted to Say's Law and the discussion of gluts. Thornton observed that if savings tended to become excessive, the supply of funds in the money market would rise relative to demand and the interest rate would fall. The lowered interest rates would both encourage investment and discourage savings, the process continuing until the two were equal. In other words, any funds not used for consumption would find their way into investment. Changes in the rate of interest would insure that savings would be invested and the level of total spending maintained. There could be no surplus of savings and no general glut of commodities. Total spending on consumption and investment would then be adequate to purchase the total output of industry.

These complicated arguments were extraordinarily important. At the purely logical level they closed the theoretical system of classical economics by showing that a free market economy would utilize all its resources. In terms of social philosophy or ideology they showed that unemployment and instability were not caused by a private enterprise economy but were the result of noneconomic factors, psychological factors, or some other cause not associated with the institutional structure and natural processes of economic life. Finally, they prescribed a policy treatment for whatever depressions might occur: (1) strengthen the financial sector of the economy so that the processes of savings and investment could work themselves out; (2) endure the crisis until declining wages and prices ultimately encouraged enough investment to bring the economy back to normal. Such is the strength of a logical and precise theory that these policies prevailed for more than a century—at tremendous social cost, for the waiting period often brought waves of bankruptcy and long-continued unemployment —until the theory was finally demolished by a countertheory propounded during the Great Depression of the 1930's.

BENTHAM AND INTERVENTIONIST LIBERALISM

No discussion of classical economics is complete without an account of the ideas of Jeremy Bentham (1748-1832). This strange Englishman, a lifelong reformer, was a nonpracticing lawyer. His *Fragment on Government*, published anonymously when he was only twenty-eight, was a brilliant attack on the traditional legal interpretation of the English constitution as antithetical to progress. He sought to show how political reform toward greater democracy would promote "the greatest good for the greatest number." The book made a sensation, but as soon as it was revealed that the author was only a young upstart and not one of the leading constitutional lawyers of the day, it was quickly dismissed. Disillusioned, Bentham began his great philosophical work, *An Introduction to the Principles of Morals and Legislation*, which was privately printed in 1780 but not published for the general public until 1789, after another of his books, *A Defense of Usury*, had been a popular success.[2]

Principles of Morals and Legislation is the key work in utilitarian philosophy. In it Bentham argued that every act was morally valuable to the extent that it resulted in happiness. Both human actions and moral judgments were based upon the poles of pleasure and pain:

> Nature has placed mankind under the governance of two sovereign masters, *pain* and *pleasure*. It is for them alone to point out what we ought to do, as well as to determine what we shall do. On the one hand the standard of right and wrong, on the other the chain of causes and effects, are fastened to their throne.

This single principle was more complex than it appeared, however. Bentham meant that the social system should seek to maximize its total welfare and distribute it as widely as possible. A small increase in happiness for many was better than a large increase for a few, in his opinion. But, as critics were to point out, that conclusion is not self-evident.

An important problem it raised was that of measurement. Increasing human happiness involves choosing among alternatives, and the cost of one course of action is the elimination of others—that is, we can't have everything. This means that comparisons of the magnitudes of benefits and costs must be made in order to determine the best, or optimal, solutions. As long as the discussion involved only total benefits, the problem was insoluble. Not until the economists of the last quarter of the nineteenth century began analyzing *increments* in benefits and costs—the famous marginal analysis—were even partial solutions found.

A related question was whether happiness, or utility, could be quantified. Bentham thought it could, at least in principle, but others argued that only comparisons could be made—for example, "I greatly prefer Mary to Jane, but my preference for chocolate over vanilla ice cream is not very strong." The absolute amounts of happiness derived from being with Mary or eating chocolate ice cream are, according to this view, impossible to measure and, furthermore, are irrelevant to the choices made.

These fine points were less important to Bentham than was his

---

[2] Bentham's major work had been completed before he reached his fortieth birthday, but he lived to be eighty-four and to wield great influence over a small band of devoted followers. He was never again to write an influential book but spent much of his later life devising complicated plans for prison reform, poor relief, education, and legislative reform. He founded the University of London with an endowment, and his will provided that his body be embalmed and once a year seated at the meeting of the university's trustees as a reminder of the principles on which the university was established. This grisly ritual is still performed today!

argument that people, *in fact,* made decisions on the basis of the amounts of utility derived from the alternative courses of action open to them. This "hedonistic calculus" was the principle underlying all human action, he declared, and the means by which the welfare of society was maximized. He believed that the selfishness of economic behavior was natural, rational, and desirable.

At this point in the argument, Bentham brought in morals and legislation. If people always act only for their own greatest pleasure when they *should* act for the greatest happiness of all, is there not a contradiction involved? Bentham said there was not, because moral and legislative sanctions caused individual action to coincide with the public interest. The sanctions rewarded individual action that benefited all and punished action that diminished public welfare. Both morality and government action (if it was majority action) had a utilitarian foundation and rested on the principle of greatest happiness. Bentham, then, was not opposed to government action if it was based on democratic processes and did not reflect the narrow interests of special groups. At the same time, he wished to give free play to individual decision-making within the framework of moral and legislative sanctions. His goal was to reconcile individualism and social action.

Bentham's significance goes far beyond his rather narrow and outdated view of human nature. In the first place, his ideas were important throughout the nineteenth century and profoundly affected later developments in economics. His view of man as a pleasure machine, continually calculating the advantages and disadvantages of alternative courses of action, became the accepted view, and rational economic behavior was defined in those terms. The assumption that individual decisions would lead to maximum public welfare was inherent, of course, in the work of Adam Smith and the other classical economists, but Bentham made it explicit. All the later conclusions of orthodox economics were solidly based on, or at least closely related to, this concept of human nature.

Even more important than his influence on economic science was Bentham's impact on liberal social philosophy. He brought to it an interventionist emphasis quite at variance with the tradition of laissez faire, creating a problem that even today remains unsolved.

The classical liberalism of the eighteenth century emphasized individual freedom as the ultimate goal of all policy. Reacting against political centralization and economic regulation, its advocates argued that any restriction on freedom hindered the achievement of maximum welfare. At the hands of Adam Smith, its greatest explicator, this philosophy advocated minimizing the role of government, strictly limiting it to such essentials as police, justice, and arms.

Bentham, however, saw that this philosophy was based on the

assumption that only individual action could create welfare. His practical mind told him that the actions of one person in his own interest might reduce the welfare of another. His legal training and his study of constitutional law told him that the institutional arrangements within which people act could significantly determine the outcome of their actions. The very fact that human society was organized by man-made institutional arrangements—that a social system existed—meant that conscious action could create social forms which would enable men to live better lives. Benthamite utilitarianism was potentially an interventionist doctrine.

Bentham and his followers in England—they called themselves philosophical radicals—included the economists James Mill, David Ricardo, and later John Stuart Mill. Advocates of democratic government and majority rule, their major target for reform was the political system, which in their day excluded large numbers of people from the right to vote and did not provide fully for freedom of speech and the press. They believed that the social system could bring the greatest good to the greatest number only if it were fully democratic and subject to true majority rule. They were also classical economists and expounded the advantages of a freely competitive market system and of laissez-faire policies. But their utilitarian political philosophy was to have the gravest consequences for their economic theories. Once political reform was achieved, the new power of the enfranchised voter was used as an instrument of economic reform, and the laissez-faire policy was discarded. The reforms were justified in terms of individual and social welfare, and the greatest-good argument was used again and again. The classical liberalism that had stressed individualism gave place to an interventionist liberalism that emphasized social welfare, and Bentham was its apostle.

The rise of Benthamite ideas gave to economics an extraordinarily wide applicability to questions of social policy. At one extreme, it could encompass the thoroughgoing laissez-faire individualist. At the other, it could include the most dedicated social reformer. The theories and methods of scientific analysis were similar, and all sides could agree on which concepts were correct. But the assumptions and preconceptions differed, as did the conclusions. This characteristic of the mainstream of economic thought continues today and enables the good economist to arrive at objective conclusions even though other economists may legitimately disagree.

5

Socialism
and
Karl Marx

Modern socialism emerged as a response to the industrial era just as classical economics had, and just as the classical economists developed an ideology for the new order, the socialists developed a critique of it.

Some socialists were impractical, idealistic dreamers, some were hard-headed critics of the existing society and others were revolutionists, but all were united by their criticisms of the new industrial society and by their belief in common rather than private ownership of the means of production. Socialists had a different view of the nature of society than did the classical economists, arguing that the social fabric was an organic whole composed of classes, rather than independent individuals, as its essential elements. They stressed the cooperative element in man's nature, rather than the materialistic profit motive of private capitalism, and they advocated equalitarianism in place of the unequal distribution of income that prevailed. The socialists could often point to actual economic conditions—real defects in industrial capitalism—to support their arguments, and socialism became the *bête noir* of most orthodox economists.

SOCIALISM AND THE CLIMATE OF OPINION

The economic and political events of the half-century from 1775 to 1825 provide a background for an understanding of the rise of modern socialism. Of primary importance was the Industrial Revolution. It provided for substantial increases in living standards and opportunities for acquisition of great wealth on the part of businessmen. It was clear that the reasons for economic growth were industrialization, capital investment, and higher productivity and that every widening of market opportunities made still further advances possible.

To the socialist, however, industrialism had a different face. Workers in the new factories were paid low wages: although factory pay was high enough to draw labor from the countryside, unemployment in rural areas meant that workers were willing to accept very low wages. Hours of work were long, women and children were employed in substantial numbers and often in hard and dangerous jobs, factory discipline was often harsh and rigorous, and in some areas company-owned stores profited from exclusive selling rights among employees. Particularly in the textile and coal industries, competition kept selling prices low, and firms competed with each other by squeezing labor costs whenever possible.

The realities of industrial life created sharp contrasts between the growing wealth of the new industrialists and bankers and the poverty of those without property who formed the work force in the factories of the slum-ridden cities. During the "hungry forties" in England, Benjamin Disraeli wrote of "the two nations"—the rich and the poor—while Charles Dickens examined *Hard Times* and the public read Thomas Hood's pathetic poem of the sewing woman, *Song of the Shirt.*

Poverty there had always been, and rich and poor had lived side by side for ages. Man had always had to wrest a meager living from a recalcitrant nature. But industrialization promised abundance. For the first time it seemed as though it might be possible to produce everything men could want and that the great struggle for existence could be resolved. Yet the gray slums of Manchester and the black country of the coal mines told a different story. The promise and the reality were vastly different.

A similar difference between ideals and reality prevailed in politics. The French revolutionists of 1789 had proclaimed "liberty, equality, fraternity," and with that slogan the French had overthrown the privileges of the old order and marched through Europe to sweep away the last remnants of feudalism and aristocracy. The new beliefs in freedom and democracy seemed to be creating a political order of full democracy, just as the Industrial Revolution seemed to portend an end to poverty.

But the defeat of Napoleon brought reaction and repression—

and re-establishment of the old system of place and privilege. Even where parliamentary government existed, as in England and France, participation was limited to persons with property, and the working man was excluded from the vote. Democracy, apparently, was fine for the middle class but dangerous if extended to the worker.

The Industrial Revolution and the French Revolution had appeared to many as means of realizing some of the ageless and ancient ideals of Western civilization—abundance, an end to toil, and the brotherhood and equality of all men. Yet in the darkness of the post-Napoleonic reaction all this was betrayed, and postwar depressions seemed to produce even greater poverty and want than before, since the unemployed worker did not have even a small plot of land on which to grow his food. To the early socialists it was self-evident that private ownership of the means of production was the source of society's ills. Ownership of machines, factories, and other capital enabled the owner to reap rich rewards, to sit back and rake in profits while others worked. At the same time, his economic position gave him political power. In the eyes of the socialist, fifty years of social revolution had given wealth and power to a few owners of capital rather than to the great numbers of common men. Mankind as a whole had been betrayed in the interests of a few, in the opinion of the critics.

ROBERT OWEN, UTOPIAN

The humanitarian and idealistic roots of early socialism are typified in the work and writings of the Englishman Robert Owen (1771–1858). Apprenticed to a linen-draper at ten years of age, he worked at various establishments in the textile industry through his youth, including one shop which "often worked their employees from 8 A.M. to 2 A.M." After failing in business for himself, he became manager of a textile mill when only nineteen years old. Seven years later he was able to buy control of textile mills at New Lanark, in Scotland, and in 1800 he took over their active management. The former management had used children from orphanages as part of its labor supply, along with adults, many of whom were "thieves, drunkards and criminals of every sort." The work day ran from 6 A.M. to 7 P.M. for children as well as adults, and the company town was composed of wooden one-room houses. Yet the working and living conditions were not considered bad for the time.

Owen was a religious man who believed that the workers of New Lanark were evil because of their surroundings, so he decided to turn New Lanark into a model community. He took no more children from workhouses or orphanages and allowed no child under ten to work.

The working day was set at ten and one-half hours for both children and adults. He provided schools in the evening for the working children (imagine a child of ten going to school after working ten and one-half hours!) and set up nursery schools for younger ones. For his adult workers he established a "register of character" which recorded drunkenness and other delinquencies, such as illicit sexual behavior, so effectively that pubs quickly disappeared from the town and there were only twenty-eight illegitimate births in nine years. An elected committee, called "bug hunters" by the housewives, inspected domestic cleanliness once each week. A support fund for the injured, sick, and aged was established, into which workers were required to pay 1/60 of their wages. Thrift was encouraged by establishment of a savings bank and by provision of better houses for those who used the bank. Finally, Owen established a store that sold food and other products to workers, charging considerably lower prices and providing goods of higher quality than did private shopkeepers.

How could Owen do all this and still make money in the highly competitive textile industry? Apparently there were two reasons. First, his plants were located in an area of labor surplus and his wages were low: an investigating committee in 1819 reported that he paid 9s 11d (9 shillings, 11 pence—about $2.40) per week to men and 6s (about $1.50) per week to women, figures that were below average for the time. Second, even though his methods were paternalistic, the attention he paid to workers seems to have brought relatively high labor productivity. In 1819 profits were 12-1/2 per cent of the invested capital.

Owen himself recognized that the reforms at New Lanark had come from the patron rather than from the workers themselves, and that some form of industrial self-government would have to follow. He published his views in 1816 in one of the landmark books of the socialist movement, *The New View of Society,* at a time when England was debating the first factory act designed to limit the hours of work and establish a minimum age for child labor. Owen lobbied hard for the act, but failure of the bill adequately to cover child labor disappointed him, and the unwillingness of other employers to imitate the example of New Lanark drove him to more radical schemes.

He tried to establish cooperative communities, in which land was owned in common, and in 1824 came to the United States to open one at New Harmony, Indiana. But the community in America and others in England failed, with substantial financial loss to Owen. More successful were the cooperative retail stores established under Owen's leadership in England, beginning the far-flung consumers' cooperative movement that has been highly successful in England and Scandinavia and that has developed to some extent in the United States. Owen also tried to set up producers' cooperatives—groups of workers who owned the factory in which they worked — but these projects did not succeed.

Owen was a visionary who sought to reform society through worker-owned communities and enterprises in which profits were not permitted. He expected that in such communities the life of the individual would achieve a larger meaning through full integration into the cooperative life of the group. In an individualistic era, his efforts were doomed to fail. Perhaps he was right when he wrote to a business partner, "All the world is queer save thee and me, and me-thinks at times that thou art a little touched."

KARL MARX, REVOLUTIONARY

In sharp contrast to the idealistic and impractical Owen was the intense German, Karl Marx (1818 – 1883). Born and raised in the most economically advanced part of Germany, the Rhineland, and son of a petty legal official of the government, Marx displayed great intellectual ability at an early age. Sent to the universities at Bonn and Berlin, he first studied law with a view toward a governmental career, but his opposition to the autocratic governments in Germany precluded that career. The young Marx then turned to philosophy, with the goal of a professorship, but his studies of philosophy and religion at Berlin — his doctoral dissertation was on the Stoic and Epicurean roots of Christian doctrine — led him to atheism, and this barred him from a university career. So Marx went into journalism and became editor of a liberal Cologne newspaper in 1842. It was there, while writing on economic problems, that he became convinced of the economic basis of politics — that underneath political theories and political power lay the economic interests of various groups in society. His newspaper was suppressed by the government for its liberal views, however, and Marx went to Paris where he married his childhood sweetheart, the daughter of a German baron, and became acquainted with a number of socialists.

One of them was Pierre Joseph Proudhon (1809 – 1865), a socialist leader who influenced him very strongly. Proudhon's chief work was a book called *What is Property?* ("property is theft," he answered to his own question), a forceful statement of the idea that the whole product of industry should go to the worker and that private property in the means of production enabled the capitalist to appropriate wealth that rightfully belonged to the worker. This concept — not original with Proudhon — was a basic tenet of nineteenth-century socialism and fundamental to Marx' own view of capitalism. Another of Proudhon's books, subtitled *The Philosophy of Poverty,* attacked the orthodox economics of his time and especially the "iron law of wages" — the Malthusian argument that wage rates tended toward the subsistence level because of population growth. Convinced that Proudhon's arguments were specious, Marx attacked his friend in a book sarcastically titled *The Poverty of Philosophy*, and legend has it that Proudhon never spoke to Marx again.

Another socialist whom Marx met in Paris was Friedrich Engels (1820–1895), son of a wealthy German textile manufacturer who owned mills in England as well as in Germany. Marx and Engels formed a friendship that lasted until Marx' death, and the two men collaborated in developing the ideas that Marx was later to publish. Engels supported Marx and his family for most of the next thirty-five years.

While in Paris Marx continued his journalistic career, writing articles especially critical of Prussia, and he was soon expelled from France at the request of the Prussian government. Moving to Brussels in 1848, just before the outbreak of the revolutions of that year, Marx and Engels wrote the *Communist Manifesto*: "A spectre is haunting Europe. . . . Workingmen of the world unite, you have nothing to lose but your chains!" Marx had entered on his career as active revolutionist.

When the revolution broke out Marx returned to Cologne, began his newspaper again, and publicized the revolution sweeping Europe. But the revolt was suppressed, and Marx, expelled from Germany and unwelcome in France, went to England, where he spent the rest of his life. He continued in journalism from time to time. For a while he was English correspondent for the New York *Tribune*, and he wrote on the French Commune of 1870 for the London *Times*. But most of his time was spent on scholarship, doing research on economics in the library of the British Museum and writing his great work, *Capital*. This book was both a denunciation of capitalism—Marx invented the word—and an explanation of why it must fail. The first volume appeared in 1867 and was the only part completed by Marx himself. The second volume appeared in 1885, two years after Marx' death, and was edited by Engels, while the last part was not issued until 1894.

Scholarship did not completely replace revolutionary agitation, however, for when the International—an international alliance of revolutionary parties—was formed in 1864, Marx took a leading part. It was not enough to be a theorist, he felt, for there had to be a revolutionary party to take control when capitalism collapsed. He wrote extensively in support of the proletarian revolutionary movement and in opposition to socialists whose views differed from his own. Marx set a precedent in the use of vitriolic denunciation which has continued to plague left-wing radicalism to the present day.

Marx died in 1883 after having given to revolutionary socialism its theoretical foundations. One wonders how different the world might be today had not the rigid authoritarianism of post-Napoleonic

Prussia barred Marx from a career in government or the universities.

THE BREAKDOWN OF CAPITALISM

Marx believed that capitalism was doomed, and he developed an intricate analysis of the "laws of motion" of capitalist society to prove it. At one level the argument has a moral basis: the inherent injustices of capitalism lead ultimately to economic and social conditions that cannot be maintained. At another level the argument is sociological: class conflict—between a decreasing number of increasingly wealthy capitalists and a growing and increasingly miserable working class—will lead ultimately to social revolution. And finally, the argument is economic: the accumulation of capital in private hands makes possible economic abundance yet also leads to the economic breakdown of capitalism. At each level the idea of conflict is emphasized, conflict between ideal and reality, between capital and labor, between growth and stagnation. Out of conflict comes change, and for this basic reason, according to Marx, capitalism must give way to another form of society in which conflict is replaced by ethical, social, and economic harmony. Change is the "dialectical process" by which socialism was ultimately to replace capitalism. Marx felt that the whole process had an economic basis in the division of society into workers and capitalists. Their relationship was exploitive, with the owners of the means of production having the upper hand. Conflict was inherent in this situation, he argued, and it would build up until the whole fabric of society was torn apart.

It is difficult to condense this grand scheme of Marx' thought without doing injustice to the power and consistency of his reasoning. The very fact that Marx' argument is long and intricate, with all parts of it logically connected and integrated, makes almost any short summary a falsification. Nevertheless, it is important that it be understood, if only because it is the basis of one of the most powerful ideologies in the modern world.

Marx begins with the idea that labor in a capitalist economy is exploited: it is not paid the full value of the products and services it produces. The capitalist employs the worker at the current wage rate and works him for as many hours each day as he can, making sure that the value of the worker's output is greater than the wage paid to him. It is this difference between wage and output value that Marx called "surplus value" and that becomes the capitalist's profit. Exploitation of the worker can be intensified, and the surplus value appropriated by the capitalist increased, by an employer's efforts to achieve lower wages, longer hours, and employment of a greater number of women and children. Thus Marx explained some of the more widely prevalent characteristics of the industrial economy of his time.

But, he continued, the labor market itself will determine the level of wage rates, while hours of work are limited by human endurance and employment of women and children is affected by a combination of technological factors and labor market conditions. The employer has relatively little flexibility in these matters and cannot readily gain a competitive advantage over other capitalists except by reinvesting the surplus value he earns in new machinery and equipment, which raise the productivity of his labor and increase his profits still further. Indeed, he is compelled to do so if he wishes to survive, because his competitors will do the same. In this way Marx explained the process of capital accumulation and the growing productivity and increased output that it generates.

However, said Marx, although capital accumulation is the great force leading to progress, it is also, together with inadequate purchasing power, one of the twin causes of the breakdown of the system. Both conditions arise from exploitation of labor, and both lead ultimately to social revolution. When the economy is prosperous, business firms earn surplus value for their owners and reinvest it for expanded output. But purchasing power eventually lags because workers are not paid the full value of their labor, and sooner or later a glut of unsold commodities appears on the market. Production is then cut back and prices fall: unemployment increases, surplus value (profit) declines and then disappears, and capital accumulation is halted. The capitalist "crisis" continues until the glut of commodities has been disposed of, prices recover, surplus value reappears, and capital accumulation resumes, continuing until the next glut appears. This process, argued Marx, creates the recurring cycles of prosperity and depression that are an inherent failing of capitalism.

Marx also argued that the crises would become more severe —longer and deeper—as capitalism developed, because the total capital and productive capacity of the economy would increase from crisis to crisis, causing the gluts to become larger and larger, to take longer and longer to be disposed of, and to necessitate greater and greater cutbacks in production.

But why, one might ask, will the glut appear in the first place? Will not rising prosperity cause increases in employment, wage rates, and purchasing power? Marx answered that even during prosperity the army of the unemployed receives recruits—workers whose jobs are taken over by machines. Capital investment leads to substitution of capital for labor. Indeed, this is the only way in which the capitalist can increase the rate at which he accumulates surplus value. During prosperity, therefore, capital accumulation creates technological unemployment and pushes wages and purchasing power down, just as commodity gluts do during periods of depression. In either case, the result is the immiseration of the working class.

This is only half of the picture, however. Changes also take place within the capitalist class. First of all, the rate of profit declines as the businessman's investment in machinery and equipment gradually becomes an increasing proportion of his total investment. (Marx was thoroughly convinced of this when he wrote the first volume of *Capital*, but the notes he left for volume three showed that he was not quite so sure that profit rates must necessarily decline as capital accumulation proceeded.) Second, the business cycles engendered by capitalism enable the big capitalists to gobble up the little ones. The firms with the largest financial resources survive, and over the years the ownership of industry gradually becomes centralized in fewer and fewer hands until a few great financiers control all. This remaining capitalist class becomes increasingly wealthy, in contrast to the growing misery of the proletariat, which expands as small businessmen fail and join its ranks. Ultimately the revolution occurs, a popular uprising of the vast majority against the wealthy few. Led by Communists, the working class seizes power and proceeds to build the new society. The process of capitalist development from exploitation to revolution is outlined in Figure 1.

THE MARXIST VISION

Marx' analysis of capitalist development was based on the assumption that two great forces are continually at work in the development of human society. One is the struggle of man against nature to obtain subsistence and ease. The development of technology and improvements in methods of production is one result of that struggle, and in its early stages capitalism represented a major step toward abundance. Factory production and machine technology greatly increased man's command over nature, and the competitive nature of capitalism forced businessmen continually to reinvest their profits in new and better methods of production. Capitalism's failure lay in its inability to continue this process and in the periodic breakdowns, or crises, that occurred.

In Marx' view, the struggle for existence led to the second great force that causes economic and social change: the struggle of man against man. Human beings are one type of productive resource, and control over men is one way in which a few can increase their wealth and welfare. Therefore, argued Marx, the struggle for existence inevitably leads to exploitation of man by man. The first manifestations of this principle were the patriarchal family and then the slave-based economy of ancient times, which gave way ultimately to serfdom. That, in turn, developed into the wage system of capitalism.

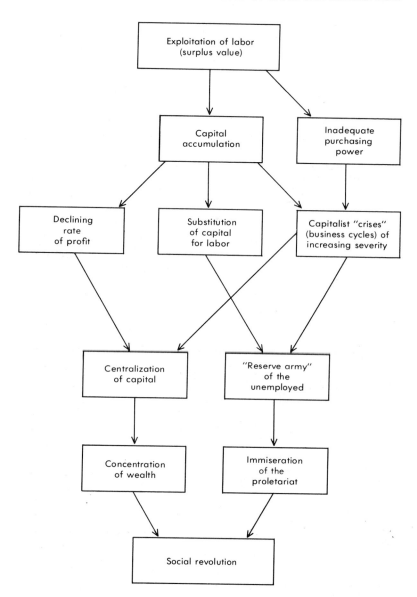

Figure 1   **SCHEMATIC DIAGRAM OF MARX' THEORY OF CAPITALIST DEVELOPMENT**

Exploitation of labor (surplus value)

Capital accumulation

Inadequate purchasing power

Declining rate of profit

Substitution of capital for labor

Capitalist "crises" (business cycles) of increasing severity

Centralization of capital

"Reserve army" of the unemployed

Concentration of wealth

Immiseration of the proletariat

Social revolution

According to Karl Marx, the injustices of capitalism embodied in exploitation of the working class by capitalists must end — by an inexorable process of development — in a complete breakdown of the social and economic order and in social revolution.

Each of these stages in social development represented a victory in the battle against nature and marked an increase in human freedom—for some, if not all—and each was made possible by advances in technology and the "social organization" of production, to use Marx' term.

Ultimately, he argued, the economy could achieve widespread abundance and produce enough for all, and at this point in human history all men could be completely free, both politically and economically. Capitalism could not achieve this goal because it prevented the full development of modern technology, resulted in the periodic stoppage of capital accumulation, and created the conditions of social revolution. But socialism could achieve the goal because it eliminated exploitation and class distinctions and because it removed the roadblocks hindering the advance of production.

Marx concluded that an economy of abundance was possible only in a classless society. When the abundant economy arrived, there would no longer be any need for social or economic differences, and exploitation would long before have ended. Distribution of income would be based on the maxim "From each according to his abilities, to each according to his needs." At this point the two great struggles of mankind—man against nature and man against man—would be ended. This was the positive side of Marxism—its vision of a great world of abundance, equality, and freedom.

WAS MARX WRONG?

One of the least useful economic debates of the twentieth century has been over the correctness of Marx' analysis of capitalism. As proof of Marx' errors, his detractors point to the rising living standards of modern nations. The working class has not been subjected to growing misery, and labor unions have gained economic and political power in all the major industrialized countries. Moreover, the working class has shared the increased wealth, income, and economic benefits that have been spread widely throughout all social classes.

Marxists answer that the extremes of exploitation have been shifted from the domestic working class to that of colonial areas. Peoples dominated politically or economically by great capitalist nations now bear the greatest burden of exploitation, enabling the capitalists to ease their treatment of the working class at home and allow its living standards to rise. They also point to the continuing extremes of poverty and wealth within nations, to the rise of big business and the prevalence of monopoly, to the significant influence wielded in politics by business interests, and to the failure of capitalist nations to find a cure for depressions and unemployment as indications that the Marxist analysis was essentially correct. In spite of all the "concessions" that have been made to the working class—social welfare legislation, union organization, higher living standards—the Marxists contend that the basic defects of capitalism remain, holding back economic growth and postponing indefinitely the emergence of the abundant society.

Yet even if the Marxist predictions of increased misery and a polarized society were proven wrong, Marx' arguments must give us pause. No society can long endure that excludes a substantial group of its citizens from enjoying its benefits, as was the case for many workingmen and their families in Marx' day and during the nineteenth-century decades of discontent and potential upheaval in Europe. In many respects Marx' analysis was a theoretical interpretation of actual conditions.

In the years after 1870, however, many great changes took place on the European scene. The right to vote—political democracy—was gradually extended to working people. National systems of welfare legislation provided protection against the worst effects of the industrial system. The growth of labor unions, and in Europe the appearance of labor's political parties, gave a new dignity to the worker and signified the place industrial labor was making for itself. The "safety valve" of emigration to North and South America and to Australia enabled many dissatisfied Europeans to start a new life in freer societies. And imperialism offered significant economic opportunities, whatever else might be said against it.

Social tensions would not have been sufficiently eased, however, in spite of these developments, without growth in the European economy. Industrialism opened many doors to the intelligent, ambitious man—Robert Owen is only one example. Although it has always been true that one gets ahead more easily if he begins near the top, it is equally true that a growing and changing economy offers more opportunities than a stagnant one. Continued economic growth, both external and internal, gave Europe time to adapt to the stresses of industrialization by instituting reforms that gave political rights to workers and protected them from the harshest effects of the market economy. One moral to be derived from Marxism is that an economy must provide dignity and wide opportunities for all if society is to remain healthy.

Chapter

6

The Philosophy
of
Individualism

The rise of socialism and its demand for social justice forced the supporters of the existing order to raise their defenses. A theoretical refutation was also needed, because Marx' critique of capitalism was based on the assumptions of classical economics itself—on the labor theory of value and the theory of capital accumulation. He used the weapons of the dominant ideology to attack the very system those weapons defended.

One answer to Marx and socialism was the nineteenth-century philosophy of individualism, which developed as the ideology of a business civilization in the years between 1850 and the First World War. Just as Marxism had carried the disenchantment of the dispossessed and the alienated to a high level of theoretical analysis, so a revived and reinforced theory of laissez faire expressed the interests of the successful. Few of the protagonists of the new individualism could be called economists in the strict sense of the word—the most important were philosophers, jurists, and businessmen—but their economic thought left a far greater impact on their world than did the work of hundreds of academicians.

The second reaction to Marx was a reconstruction of economics itself, accomplished by stripping away its weak elements, strengthening its scientific validity, generalizing its basic concepts, and adapting it to the contemporary world. Economics as a science was greatly strengthened by the impact of socialist theory and criticism. But the tenor of the times and the climate of opinion within which the reconstructed economics emerged were set by other, more practical men of affairs.

THE PHILOSOPHY

An English philosopher, Herbert Spencer (1820–1903), and an American sociologist, William Graham Sumner (1840–1910), led the further development of the philosophy of individualism. These men worked out the ideology on which half a century of legislation, law, and folklore was based.

Spencer was an evolutionist before Darwin. As early as 1850, in his *Social Statics*, he maintained that all social systems develop and change by a natural process that results in a maximization of individual welfare. This process of natural development stems from competition among individuals, he argued, and any interference on the part of the government prevents full achievement of the ideal goal. Spencer's early statement was followed by essays and a ten-volume *Synthetic Philosophy*, which sought to show that evolutionary progress occurred in all phenomena—in the biological world, in the human mind, in society, and in ethics. Where Darwin explained evolution in terms of "natural selection," Spencer invented the phrase "survival of the fittest" as the source of progress.

Any organism, including the social, changes through adaptation to outside influences, carried out in such a way as to benefit the organism involved.

Those organisms which are best fitted to their environment, or which change to fit themselves to their environment, will survive. The least fit will die out, leaving the strongest and "best."

In this way progress is made, and the weakest individuals and the least useful social institutions gradually are eliminated. Since the individual member of society is the decision-maker, the social organization that emerges from the process of change is more closely adapted to meeting the needs of the individual. Progress means that the welfare of the individual must be improved.

These ideas led to a description of the ideal society, conceived as static equilibrium between man and his surroundings brought about by full exercise of man's natural rights. Government, a necessary evil, was severely limited to protection of man and his property and enforcement of private contracts—nothing else. As society moved from a primitive state of violence and military control to higher levels of industrialization and peace, even the protective role of government could be reduced and would ultimately wither away in the final utopia of philosophical anarchism. In the transition, however, there should be no government regulation of industry, no state church, no organized colonization, no relief for the poor, no social legislation, no public mint, no government-owned postal system, no public education. Unfettered individual action should be permitted, and nothing should be allowed to interfere with natural selection of the fittest—not even such measures as public sanitation, which protected and thereby perpetuated weaker types.

Spencer's philosophy had a greater impact in the United States than in his own country. His foremost American follower was William Graham Sumner, an Episcopalian minister and Yale University economist who became one of the foremost sociologists of his time. His major work is a sociological classic, *Folkways* (1907), which examined social "mores"—institutions and conventions that develop and continually change by a process of adaptation to individual and social needs. If such institutions do not contribute to welfare and survival, they are gradually replaced by more effective methods, and the social system evolves into a higher and better form. Social institutions which have proved their usefulness in the past are given up only with reluctance, however, and only after new methods have been proven better. In Sumner's view, therefore, the social system is at one and the same time conservative and progressive, resistant to change and changing.

Within the social system, individuals are also rising and falling, according to Sumner. The man with ability, intelligence, and drive will rise to prominence by competing with his fellows. The lazy, ignorant, and weak man will fall out of sight. The emergence of leading individuals brings progress, because these are the men who innovate, who think, who develop new ideas. Competition among them results in both a more vigorous population and a better social structure.

In a long series of essays with such titles as "What Social Classes Owe to One Another," "The Forgotten Man," and "The Concentration of Wealth: Its Economic Justification," Sumner applied his theory of society to questions of contemporary policy. "The Forgotten Man" was the man who worked hard, produced, paid his taxes, saved, and invested, and thereby brought to society all the benefits of his work and enterprise, in spite of bearing the burden of protective tariffs, government social services, and the high costs imposed by labor unions.[1] Concentrated wealth was justified because it was used to produce for others. Wealth that was squandered or allowed to lie idle never led

---

[1]Ironically, Sumner's phrase "the forgotten man" was reversed by Franklin Roosevelt and used to describe the poor and downtrodden who would benefit by the welfare measures of the New Deal, an interventionist program that Sumner would have abhorred.

to such concentration. The economic elite rose to the top only because, in competition with others, they expanded economic activity and produced the goods and services that society wanted and needed. Social classes owed nothing to one another; they had only to look out for themselves, and benefits to others would automatically follow.

This, then, was evolutionary philosophy applied to the social system. It justified unlimited individualism on the ground that only social good could come from competition. It justified great wealth on the ground that wealth existed only because it served others. It justified lack of responsibility for others on the ground that anyone destroyed by competition could be considered "unfit," not capable of making a large enough contribution to the social order to survive. It was a rigorous philosophy that associated success with right and failure with wrong, wealth with public service and poverty with uselessness.

INDIVIDUALISM AND THE LAW

In the United States the philosophy of unrestricted individualism came to be embodied in our fundamental constitutional law. The man most responsible for this development was a now almost forgotten justice of the United States Supreme Court, Stephen J. Field (1816–1899). Field was the son of a prominent Congregational clergyman and the brother of two equally eminent men, Cyrus Field, the businessman who laid the first trans-Atlantic telegraph cable in 1866, and David Dudley Field, a prominent New York lawyer who led the movement for reform of legal codes in the 1860's and who later became the leader of an international movement to substitute arbitration for war, a forerunner of The League of Nations.

In his early thirties Stephen Field joined the gold rush to California. He was elected a judge and in 1850 to the state legislature. By 1857 he was on the state supreme court and became its chief justice in 1859. Field was a product of the developing West and its individualistic, open social structure in which a man could rise through his own efforts.

Abraham Lincoln appointed him to the United States Supreme Court in 1863, a position he held for thirty-four years, becoming one of the country's greatest authorities on constitutional law. In 1876 he was a member of the famous Electoral Commission that decided the presidency in favor of the Republican Rutherford B. Hayes against the Democrat Samuel J. Tilden, who had a larger total vote. During his career on the Supreme Court, Field's most important opinions related to protection of property and freedom of business enterprise, by application to corporations of the Fourteenth Amendment to the Constitution. At first in the minority, Field soon became the most important majority spokesman for the view that the Constitution guarantees individual and business enterprise against government intervention.

The famous Slaughterhouse Cases of 1873 enabled Field to state his position in unequivocal terms. Louisiana had passed laws intending to protect public health in New Orleans by limiting the operation of slaughterhouses and giving a monopoly of the business to a single company. The act was opposed by butchers and cattle dealers who asked for an injunction against enforcement on the grounds that the act was unconstitutional. They argued, among other things, that the monopoly deprived them of the right to follow their usual employment and, contrary to the Fourteenth Amendment, deprived them of property without due process of law and denied them equal protection under the law. Supporters of the legislation argued that it represented a valid expression of the police power of the state government. The case was ultimately appealed to the Supreme Court, where the majority held that the state was legitimately using its police powers and that no civil rights had been violated. Field, however, wrote a vigorous dissent. He felt that the right to operate a slaughterhouse or any other legitimate business enterprise was a right that could not be removed by government. "I cannot believe that what is termed in the Declaration of Independence a God-given and inalienable right can thus be ruthlessly taken from citizens, or that there can be any abridgement of that right except by regulations alike affecting all persons of the same age, sex and condition."

The argument for property as a natural right that no government can appropriate without due process of law was tested further in the ensuing years. Field dissented vigorously on several occasions when the majority of the Supreme Court supported state intervention in economic affairs. But opinion changed, and by 1886 the whole Court had come to accept Field's position. In a case concerning the validity of special taxes imposed on the Southern Pacific Railway by a California county, Field could say, "The Court does not want to hear the argument on the question whether the provision of the 14th amendment applies to these corporations. We are all of the opinion that it does." The constitutional amendment that originally had been intended to protect freed slaves was then applied to corporations and to business enterprise, and in this case the local taxes were declared invalid.

Once Field's position became part of the constitutional law of the United States, much state legislation was stricken down, including regulation of hours of work, child labor, factory conditions, and other aspects of economic life. At a time when industrial growth was creating many new problems, the philosophy of unrestricted laissez faire was the law of the land, and little interference with private enterprise and freedom of contract was permitted. In vain did Justice Oliver Wendell Holmes complain in one famous dissenting opinion that "the four-teenth amendment does not enact Mr. Herbert Spencer's *Social Statics.*"

THE FOLKLORE OF INDIVIDUALISM

The philosophy of individualism was translated into a folklore as well as legal principles. The lore told of the poor immigrant boy who started his career at the bottom of the business ladder, worked hard, saved his money, made shrewd investments, and ultimately rose to a position of business leadership. He married well, raised a happy family, and gained the respect of his fellows. Wise in his old age, he was an elder statesman consulted by Presidents and loved by his grand-children.

Although relatively few business leaders followed this path to the top—most were sons of business or professional men, had more than an average education, and did not start at the bottom—a growing economy in which individual enterprise was unhindered and which had no income taxes did offer a fertile field to the man bent on riches. A few men actually were living examples of the folklore, although they did not rise within existing enterprises but built their own busi-nesses with shrewdness, ability, and luck.

Andrew Carnegie, for example, was born in Scotland, son of a weaver who brought his family to America when power looms forced him out of business. The thirteen-year-old Andrew went to work in a textile plant near Pittsburgh as a bobbin boy at twenty cents a day. His hard work earned him a promotion to the engine room, and his knowledge of arithmetic and his penmanship earned him another promotion to the clerical staff. Seeking newer fields with greater op-portunity, Andrew became a telegraph messenger boy, learned teleg-raphy, became an operator, and in his spare time earned extra money as a newspaper telegraph reporter. Moving again to greener fields, he became a telegraph train dispatcher for the Pennsylvania Railroad and then secretary to the general superintendent. When his boss became president of the company, Andrew, then all of twenty-five years old, was appointed superintendent of the railroad's western division. Saving his money, he invested in a sleeping-car company and in oil lands, two new and dynamic industries at the time. During the Civil War Carnegie was in charge of all the eastern military railroads and telegraphs, and he ran them with the efficiency he had applied to all of his work.

Forecasting the superiority of iron and steel bridges over those made of wood, he organized the Keystone Bridge Works in 1862. Shortly after the Civil War ended he built his own steel plant to supply raw material to his company and in 1868 introduced the Bessemer steel process into the United States. Building and expanding further, he acquired more plants, iron and coal mines, railroads, and all the other elements of the first fully integrated steel company in the country. Rather than run it himself, he took care to hire the best managerial talent available and gave his managers incentives to work with initiative and progressiveness. In 1901 he sold his company to the newly formed United States Steel Corporation for almost half a billion dollars. Carnegie himself received over $300 million.

Carnegie believed and lived the philosophy that wealth is held by the individual only as a stewardship and that it is to be used ultimately for the benefit of society as a whole. After selling his company, he devoted the remainder of his life to supporting education and research. He established and financed the Carnegie Institute of Technology in Pittsburgh, the Carnegie Institution of Washington for purposes of scientific research, the Carnegie Corporation of New York as a trust fund for support of education and research, the Carnegie Foundation for the Advancement of Teaching, the Carnegie Endowment for International Peace, and the Carnegie Hero Fund to provide rewards for heroic deeds, in addition to endowing libraries in hundreds of cities across the country. In all of these gifts he insisted on the principle of self-help: the recipient almost always had to provide some money himself.

Carnegie wrote several popular books expressing his philosophy of individualism and stewardship of wealth: *Triumphant Democracy* (1886), *The Gospel of Wealth* (1900), and *The Empire of Business* (1902). All of these works extolled the business system, individualism, free enterprise, and the idea that wealth was not to be used solely for individual benefit but devoted to community betterment. Typical of his opinions was an article on "Wealth" published in the *North American Review* in 1889.

> The price which society pays for the law of competition . . . is also great; but the advantages of this law are also greater still, for it is to this law that we owe our wonderful material development, which brings improved conditions in its train.
> . . . While the law may be sometimes hard for the individual, it is best for the race, because it insures the survival of the fittest in every department.

Accumulation of wealth by the few can lead to a "reign of harmony" and "reconciliation of the rich and the poor" as long as the wealthy use their riches "as a matter of duty" in the ways "best calculated to produce the most beneficial results for the community."

The laws of accumulation will be left free; the laws of distribution free. Individualism will continue, but the millionaire will be but a trustee for the poor; intrusted for a season with a great part of the increased wealth of the community, but administering it for the community far better than it could or would have done for itself.

Andrew Carnegie was a living embodiment of a folklore of individualism which maintained that private property was a natural element of the social order, obtained by industry and thrift and demonstrating the moral superiority of its possessors. As Russell Conwell, a famous public speaker of the time, put it in his inspirational piece "Acres of Diamonds," "Godliness is in league with riches." Or as the Episcopalian bishop William Lawrence said, "In the long run it is only to the man of morality that wealth comes." By contrast, poverty was the result of laziness, or waste, or lack of ability—desirable only because it taught the need for hard work and saving. This philosophy was not merely a rationalization of wealth by the wealthy, although it was certainly that. But it was also the faith of millions, including the great middle class and a large number of workers.

RESULTS OF INDIVIDUALISM

Individualism also had its seamy side. The apologists for wealth had much to apologize for. In 1900, when profits of the Carnegie Steel Company were more than $20 million for the year (most of it going to Andrew Carnegie himself), the average *annual* wage for steel workers was about $600. The justice of this division of society's income was not self-evident, and it threatened the polarization of social classes that Marx had railed against. Yet the more extreme adherents of the philosophy of laissez faire went merrily on their way, apparently unaware of the potentially explosive situation they were creating.

At one time, when the New York Central Railroad canceled a fast extra-fare train between New York and Chicago, a public outcry was raised. Interviewed by a newspaper reporter, William Vanderbilt, the company's president and majority stockholder, exploded, "The public be damned. I am working for my stockholders. If the public want the train why don't they pay for it?" The statement raised a storm of protest; Vanderbilt decided it was time to diversify his interests and sold $30 million of his Central stock.

It was a great age for the speculator, the promoter, and the freebooter. In 1869, Jay Gould and Jim Fisk, financial speculators who had learned their trade through almost certainly illegal watering of Erie Railroad stock, attempted to corner the free gold supply in the

New York money market. Tying up the federal government's gold supply in the New York subtreasury by bringing President Grant's brother-in-law into the plot, they drove the price of gold to great heights. Their Washington connections brought advance warning of government action to break the corner, and they sold out in time to make large profits. When a financial panic ensued, they even allowed their own brokers to be bankrupted. This Black Friday of September 24, 1869, was only the most spectacular of the speculative games that unsettled the economy from time to time.

The builders of monopoly were also at work. The new industrial economy was particularly vulnerable to competitive price wars. In the railroad industry, for instance, capital costs were high, and rate cutting could bring returns down to well below total costs while still covering operating expenses. Rate wars could bankrupt the weaker lines, but, since railroad property could be used only for running trains, defeated companies would merely reorganize on a stronger financial basis and return to the industrial wars better able to survive than the lines which had won out the first time. It is little wonder that railroad companies merged, arranged agreements on rates and division of traffic, bought stock interests in one another, and formed "communities of interest."

Similar factors were at work in other industries as well: steel, agricultural equipment, sugar refining, oil refining and distribution, and public utilities. Giant trusts were formed to bring stability into industries made chaotic by the very competition that the theorists had claimed was the basis of economic order. In combining, financiers sometimes lost sight of economic benefits to company, stockholders, or public when large fees for legal and financial services beckoned. When J. P. Morgan began building large steel companies out of small ones in the 1890's, he discovered that issuing securities in amounts larger than the real value of the merged properties could bring high rewards. Capitalizing "good will" and potential monopoly profits could put money into the hands of bankers and lawyers. When Andrew Carnegie threatened to wreck the scheme by sharp competition, Morgan was forced to buy him out at Carnegie's price. The United States Steel Corporation was born, with stocks and bonds sold to the public and distributed to the promoters at prices equal to about twice the real value of the properties. The company's monopoly position enabled it ultimately to carry through, but the public paid through high prices for steel. Shortly after the Carnegie-Morgan deal was closed, the two men met on an ocean voyage. Carnegie is reported to have said, "I made one mistake, Pierpont, when I sold out to you. I should have asked you $100 million more than I did." To which Morgan replied, "I should have paid it."

This kind of free-wheeling individualism engendered an inevitable reaction. In 1877 the United States came close to revolution as a result of depression and industrial discontent. Layoffs and wage reductions on the railroads triggered local strikes that spread to other lines all over the country. Violence and fighting broke out and much railroad property was destroyed. Hardly a decade later, the Haymarket Square riot erupted in Chicago. A strike at the great McCormick Reaper Works, in which union membership was a major issue, was followed by a general strike throughout the city. Over fifty thousand workers left their jobs. Agitation by "practical" anarchists, who wanted to end capitalism and all government by destructive revolution, was especially strong, and after a riot before the McCormick Works in which a number of workers were injured, the tiny anarchist newspaper called for "revenge" for the "massacre." A meeting called the next evening at Haymarket Square attracted a large crowd, and when police moved in to break up what had been a peaceful gathering, a bomb was thrown that killed seven policemen and wounded sixty-eight more. Eight anarchist leaders were arrested and tried for murder as accessories before the fact. Found guilty in a supercharged atmosphere of fear and hate, four were executed, one committed suicide in jail, and three were given long prison terms. No one ever found out who threw the bomb.

Again, in the 1890's, economic conflict bred violence. The hard times of that decade were called the "great depression"—until the 1930's. Unemployment was high, and basic industries such as steel, railroads, and agricultural equipment were hard hit. Fighting broke out in the summer of 1892 at Homestead, Pennsylvania, a steel town near Pittsburgh. Wage cuts, refusal of the company to recognize a union or to bargain with the men, and importation of several hundred strikebreakers led to a pitched battle between workers and management forces. Twenty men were killed and perhaps fifty wounded, and Henry Frick, manager of the plant, later was shot and stabbed in his office by an agitator. The National Guard finally restored order, but the strike was broken.

Near Chicago, where George Pullman had paternalistically established a "model town" next to his railroad car factory, hard times resulted in layoffs and evictions, and the workers walked out. A sympathy boycott of Pullman cars by the American Railway Union, led by Eugene Debs, tied up the nation's transportation system, and serious fighting occurred in Chicago. An injunction against the strike was obtained by the attorney general of the United States, himself a former railroad lawyer, and President Cleveland called out national troops in spite of protests from Governor Altgeld that they were not needed. In the face of this power the strike failed and Debs was jailed, to emerge a fully convinced socialist.

The conservative leaders of business seemed to learn nothing and to forget nothing, however. When a strike in the anthracite coal mines in 1902 threatened to leave big-city consumers freezing through a long winter, George F. Baer, head of the employers' association that refused the union's offer to submit the dispute to arbitration, wrote to a complaining stockholder:

> Dear Mr. Clark: I have your letter of the 16th. I do not know who you are. I see that you are a religious man; but you are evidently biased in favor of the right of the workingman to control a business in which he has no other interest than to secure fair wages. I beg of you not to be discouraged. The rights and interests of the laboring man will be protected and cared for — not by agitators — but by the Christian gentlemen to whom God has given control of the property rights of the country. Pray earnestly that the right may triumph, always remembering that the Lord God omnipotent still reigns and that this reign is one of law and order, not violence and crime.

This bald statement of the divine right of capital so aroused public opinion that the federal government finally interposed itself between the two fighting parties of capital and labor. President Theodore Roosevelt threatened to seize the mines unless management agreed to arbitrate the dispute. For the first time, intervention by the federal government was on the side of labor rather than capital.

THE LIMITATIONS OF INDIVIDUALISM

The philosophy, law, and folklore of rugged individualism was on a collision course with labor. Its refusal to deal with problems of depression and unemployment, with monopoly and concentrated economic power, with problems of income distribution and economic justice, was bringing criticism and attack. Perhaps sound in theory, it did not deal with the great issues that Marxism had raised about capitalism or with the social problems that were encountered along the path of economic development. When lack of solutions to problems resulted in upheavals and violence, public opinion began to turn the other way. Reiteration of old theories and slogans was not enough.

7

Neoclassical Economics

Economists, for the most part, did not accept the extreme position of the philosophy of individualism. They were concerned with social problems, and the influence of Benthamite utilitarianism made them willing to support government intervention in economic affairs if clear social benefits could be demonstrated. Nevertheless, most economists remained within the framework of the individualist philosophy, accepting government action only in limited amounts for limited goals. The emphasis on laissez faire remained, and economic theory reflected that point of view.

It reflected something else too: the Marxian critique of capitalism. In part consciously and in part unconsciously, the economists of 1870 to 1900 developed new theoretical formulations that served to refute the Marxist propositions about capitalism.

MARGINAL UTILITY AND INDIVIDUAL WELFARE

In the early 1870's three different economists, unaware of each other's ideas, developed a new theory of value to replace the old labor theory. An Englishman, a Frenchman, and an Austrian, they wrote in different languages, yet their theories were remarkably similar—another example of that often-observed phenomenon in the development of science, the independent and simultaneous discovery of a new principle. Within ten years the new ideas had swept triumphantly through the economics profession and had been hailed as a great breakthrough by all but a few diehards who clung obstinately to the old classical system. To compound the coincidence, the discovery came only a few years after Marx had published his attack on capitalism, using the labor theory of value as a base for his exploitation theory.

Later, it turned out that the new ideas were not so new after all. The basic principles of marginal utility had been stated by an Italian mathematician a century and a half before, and during the preceding fifty years had been published by a German engineer, a French public utilities expert, and several rather obscure English economists. Even Aristotle had used the idea in his treatise on ethics, and related concepts had been discussed by Catholic theologians in the sixteenth and seventeenth centuries. All of these writings had been ignored until Marx attacked the private-enterprise system. When that happened the labor theory of value had to go, and economists had to give serious attention to problems of income distribution and business cycles. A new approach to economics was born.

The new principle was a simple one: the value of a product or service is due not to the labor embodied in it but to the usefulness of the last unit purchased. That, in essence, was the famous principle of marginal utility.

Karl Menger (1840–1921), the Austrian codiscoverer, best stated the basic principle. He pointed out that the rational consumer, faced with a large number of alternatives on which to spend his income, will seek to maximize his satisfaction. This will be achieved when he has allocated his spending so that the last (or marginal) dollar spent on one commodity gives him no more and no less satisfaction—or welfare, or utility—than the last dollar spent on anything else he buys. If it is possible to shift a dollar of spending from one commodity to another and thereby raise the total satisfaction obtained, the rational consumer will do so, until utility "at the margin" is equalized. In this fashion the demand for any one commodity by any one consumer is determined. Menger pictured the consumer as a person who continually weighs the relative advantages of this or that course of action and always chooses the one that gives him the greatest *increment* in welfare.

William Stanley Jevons (1835–1882), the English codiscoverer, emphasized another aspect of the principle by showing that utility at the margin diminishes: the more one has of a commodity, the less satisfaction he gets from consuming one more unit and the less he is willing to pay for it. This means that plentiful commodities will be cheap because one additional unit is not worth much to the buyer, even though the commodity itself may be essential to sustain life—like water or bread. Scarce commodities, on the other hand, will be expensive because no one has many of them and one more unit will bring a great deal of satisfaction to the buyer—like diamonds or mink coats.

Léon Walras (1837–1910), the Frenchman who published the same principle in the early 1870's, had a still different emphasis. He explained how the entire economic system, including production of capital equipment and raw materials, was keyed to the spending decisions of the consumer. The economy was a seamless web of intricate relationships between prices and quantities purchased in which any change in the consumer's allocation of expenditures was felt throughout the entire system in tiny adjustments of production and prices. Especially in a competitive economy, the whole system automatically adjusted to match production to demand.

This theory of value went behind the demand for a commodity to analyze the factors on which demand was based, whereas the old labor theory of value had centered on the supply side of the market and had found value and price to be based on costs of production, which were reduced ultimately to labor. It remained for an English economist, the great Alfred Marshall (1842–1924), to reconcile these two approaches and insist that market price—that is, economic value—was determined by both supply and demand, which interact with one another in much the same way as Adam Smith described the operation of competitive markets. Marshall demonstrated that in the long run prices in competitive markets would tend toward the lowest possible costs of production at which the amounts desired by consumers would be provided. But although Marshall brought costs of production back into the picture, he and most other economists accepted the broader approach of Menger and Walras: the basic pattern of production was determined by the myriad independent decisions of millions of individual consumers.

One of the most important conclusions drawn from this line of thinking was that a system of free markets tended to maximize individual welfare. Since consumers were assumed to try to maximize their satisfactions, and since production was patterned after consumer wants, it followed that the result would be welfare maximizing. The analysis also showed that costs of production were pushed to the lowest possible level by the forces of competition. The whole economy, in a sense, was a pleasure-maximizing machine in which the difference between consumer benefits and production costs was increased to the highest level possible—if the economy were allowed to operate without constraints.

These ideas shifted the whole focus of economics away from the great issue of social classes and their economic interests, which had been emphasized by Ricardo and Marx, and centered economic theory upon the individual. The principles of income distribution, upon which Ricardo had based his analysis of the progress of industrialism and on which Marx had rested his theory of the breakdown of capitalism, were replaced by the individual consumer as the major determinant of economic activity and economic progress. The whole economic system was conceived as revolving around him and responding to his needs.

Economics was transformed into a science consistent with the social philosophy developed by Herbert Spencer and William Graham Sumner, and that philosophy, of course, reflected the free-wheeling individualism that was remaking the face of the world. The economists and their highly abstract theories were part of the same social and intellectual development that brought forth the legal theories of Stephen Field and the folklore of the self-made man.

ECONOMIC JUSTICE

The economists of the late nineteenth century also applied the marginal analysis to income distribution. Taking up the Marxist challenge, these new theologians of the industrial society developed a theory proving that all factors of production—whether labor, land, or capital—earned a wage exactly equal to their contribution to the value of output. No one could exploit anyone else, there was no unearned surplus to be appropriated by the owners of capital, and full justice must prevail in the distribution of income. The worker received what he earned, no more and no less.

The new analysis of income distribution was called the theory of marginal productivity. Like the theory of marginal utility, it was based on the last, or marginal, unit, and its fundamental conclusion was very simple: workers would be paid a wage equal to the value of the last unit of output they produced. For example, consider a single manufacturing plant that turns out only one product. This plant will pay wages equal to those established in the competitive labor market. The manager will add to his work force as long as the added output per man can be sold for more than the wage paid—that is, as long as profits rise because additional revenues exceed additional costs. The manager will stop hiring workers when increased output will not bring in enough additional revenue to cover the wage that must be paid. The plant's demand for labor is determined by the level at which wages equal the value of a worker's output at the margin. If an employer tried to pay a wage less than this value, the worker could, of course, get a job elsewhere with a competitive firm. It was a wonderful theory. The worker would get no more and no less than his contribution to society. If his productivity was high, he would earn high wages; if he was lazy or incompetent, his earnings would be low.

The same theory was applied to the boss, to profits earned on capital, and to the rent from land. Each of these elements in the production process was subject to the same economic law. No one could exploit anyone else because everyone got what he deserved. The economists even revived a theorem devised by a Swiss mathematician more than a hundred years before which proved that there could be no surplus value unaccounted for by payments to the various factors of production. Marx was dead.

The validity of the theory of marginal productivity depended upon the existence of that theoretical Nirvana, perfect competition. It also required that all factors of production be fully and freely substitutable for one another and that there be no change in costs of production per unit of output as the level of production rose or fell. But these highly restrictive assumptions did not bother many economists, who by this time were lost in the theoretical glories of a perfectly competitive economy.[1]

PROSPERITY AND DEPRESSION

Wherever large-scale industrialization appeared, the economic system was subjected to alternating periods of prosperity and depression, often marked by a "crisis" in finance and business confidence. These breakdowns occurred with varying degrees of severity but with an apparent regularity that required explanation. A timetable of the crises of the nineteenth century would look like this:

United States	England
	1815
1819	
	1825
	1836
1837	
	1847
1854	
1857	1857
	1866
1873	1873
	1882
1884	
	1890
1893	
	1900

[1]It should be noted, however, that some economists never accepted the theory of marginal productivity. This dissident group included Alfred Marshall, the dominant figure in English economics from 1890 to after World War I.

At first the problem was ignored. Both the classical economists of the first half of the century and the neoclassical group that appeared after 1870 accepted the general propositions of Say's Law of Markets, according to which there should be no periodic economic breakdowns and the economy should continue to operate at uninterrupted high levels of output and employment. Those few who did investigate business cycles looked for causes outside the system of production and distribution, for Say's Law taught that demand was created by production and that, in the aggregate, the two could never get out of phase with one another.

Beginning in the 1860's British and French statisticians, rather than economists, first verified the periodic and cyclical nature of economic fluctuations. They identified several cycles of about ten years' duration and speculated on possible causes. Stanley Jevons in England was one of the few economists who gave much attention to the problem, and he attributed the causes of "great irregular fluctuations" to variations in agriculture, excessive investment or speculation, wars and political disturbances, or "other fortuitous occurrences which we cannot calculate upon, or allow for." Later Jevons developed a theory even more favorable to the adherents of Say's Law and the existing scheme of things. After finding a statistical correlation between cycles of sun spots and business fluctuations, he wrote in 1884:

> It seems probable that commercial crises are connected with a periodic variation of weather affecting all parts of the earth, and probably arising from increased waves of heat received from the sun at average intervals of ten years and a fraction.

But business cycles were creating problems for government, too, and hard-headed administrators responsible for policy need facts, not theories. Government men sat down to analyze the data, and in 1886 Carroll Wright, in his first annual report as United States Commissioner of Labor, identified business investment as the most important fluctuating element in the economy. Natural causes, wars, and speculation were not the cause of crises: the culprit was overinvestment in capital equipment. Bad times came when opportunities for investment were inadequate. This emphasis on the process of investment was reiterated a few years later by Sir Hubert Llewellyn Smith, Wright's English counterpart as Commissioner of Labour in the Board of Trade, who reported to Parliament in 1895 that economic instability was concentrated in a few industries, such as machinery and other metals-producing industries, shipbuilding, construction, and mining, all of which were subject to "violent oscillation" in investment. Other sectors of the economy were relatively stable, and fluctuations there reflected the larger changes taking place in unstable industries.

These investigations by government servants did not have much effect on economists, however, who continued to pursue the clues given them by Say's Law. In its best and most complete formulation that law utilized the rate of interest as the automatic stabilizer of the economy, as the factor which ensured that savings would be directed into investment and prevent any break in the even flow of spending. But since breaks were obviously occurring and since the rate of interest was part of the monetary system, it was logical to look to that sector of the economy for the causes: there could be problems in the monetary system even though production and distribution were sound.

By the last decade of the nineteenth century, economists began to agree that business cycles were caused by unwarranted expansion of the money supply. Easy credit would bring interest rates down and thereby stimulate excessive investment and speculation. Once the economy had overexpanded, a crisis was inevitable, since the normal operation of the system could not support the unnecessary production capacity and credit created during the wave of optimism. Once the crisis began, the economy would simply have to suffer until the high prices and unwise expansion were brought back to normal.

The preventive for this unfortunate sequence of events was to manage the monetary system properly. Limiting the expansion of credit to the legitimate needs of business through effective action by the central bank could prevent the process from starting or could stop it while the ensuing readjustment period might still be short and shallow. Stability in the monetary and credit system could bring stability to the economy as a whole.

This theory was spelled out by the Englishman Walter Bagehot as early as 1873 in *Lombard Street*, a classic work on the money markets. It was taught at Harvard around the turn of the century by Oliver M. W. Sprague, one of whose students was the young Franklin D. Roosevelt (who fortunately did not learn the lesson well). It was the theoretical basis for the establishment of the Federal Reserve System in this country in 1914. President Herbert Hoover had this theory in mind when he said, shortly after the 1929 stock market crash, "The fundamental business of the country—that is, production and distribution—is sound." He didn't mention the monetary and credit system, which obviously was not sound and which he tried to strengthen by loans to banks and railroads (whose bonds were owned heavily by the large banks) and by trying to cut federal expenditures. But Hoover's policies pointed up the bias inherent in Say's Law of Markets and in the theory of business cycles it spawned. Production and distribution were *not* sound in 1929, even though the theory denied that causes and remedies could be found and applied in those areas.

THE IDEOLOGY OF CAPITALISM

The new economics ushered in after 1870 struck a responsive chord and within twenty years became the accepted, orthodox approach. It developed a new theory of value that was based upon individual welfare rather than labor and was stated in the logic of individual rational action. It used a new technique — marginal analysis — which led to a new explanation of income distribution. Associated with these ideas was an analysis of money and economic fluctuations based on the assumption that full employment was the normal economic condition. Together these three theories — marginal utility, marginal productivity, and the monetary theory of business cycles — supplemented the basic analysis of classical economics to picture a free-enterprise economy that produced what consumers wanted and therefore maximized welfare, distributed products justly, and normally operated at full employment levels. The mechanics of the self-adjusting market, with its price mechanism and profit-maximizing producer, were explained essentially as they had been by the classical economists. Economic growth through saving and capital accumulation were still the sources of progress. By eliminating the older theories of rent, wages, and profits, the implications of social conflict inherent in Ricardian economics were replaced by the harmonies and justice of the marginal productivity theory. It was a great and lovely vision, similar in essence to that of Adam Smith but much more advanced.

Unlike the social Darwinism of Spencer, Sumner, Field, and Carnegie, however, neoclassical economics was not a rigorous laissez-faire theory. One major exception was in the area of monetary policy, where responsibility for maintaining economic stability through proper management of the money supply was assigned to government acting through the central bank. But even in this area, policy discretion was to be limited: the criterion for monetary policy was that it limit expansion of credit to the legitimate needs of business — that is, to the needs of production and distribution. Both of those aspects of the economy were to be governed by the free play of market forces unhampered by government intervention. In the last analysis, what little monetary intervention was allowed was to be largely indicated by the free market.

Other types of intervention were also approved by most neoclassical economists. One was the effort to preserve competition by what in this country came to be called "antitrust" laws. Since their theories were based on the assumption of perfect competition in all markets, the economists were at least consistent when they argued for regulation of "natural" monopolies and for laws to prevent restraint of trade. Their commitment to competition and their support of antimonopoly legislation were not complete, however. Some economists argued that private monopolies, unsustained by government restrictions on competition, would inevitably fall from their positions of power because of efforts of other businessmen to get a share of the excessive profits. Others wanted to move slowly for fear that antitrust action might reduce the advantages to be obtained from mass production. In spite of these relatively mild dissents, however, a fairly consistent emphasis on the advantages of competition was developed and has been sustained to this day.

Still other concessions to government intervention were made. For example, Henry Sidgwick, a prominent English economist, in a paper given in 1886 before the Economic Section of the British Association for the Advancement of Science, listed a number of "economic exceptions to laissez faire." They included actions based on moral considerations, such as sanitary regulations, control of narcotics and intoxicants, and restrictions on gambling; efforts to improve the productivity of individuals by education; measures that require total public participation for effectiveness, such as public health measures and flood control; and provision of services whose benefits are general and for which the individual cannot be charged, such as lighthouses on rocky shores or certain types of scientific research. No one of these exceptions seems especially significant to the modern mind, accustomed to almost a hundred years of growing government activity, but they do point up the fact that much of neoclassical economics represented accommodations to existing needs and that it was not the simple paean to individualism and laissez faire its critics sometimes made it out to be. Many neoclassical economists could look upon their discipline as a scientific and rational path to reform.

The new economics, however, had strong ideological implications. It was a complete answer to Marx. Where the classical economists had used the labor theory of value to justify private property, Marx had used it as the basis for his theory of exploitation. Once Marx had written his devastating attack on capitalism, it was inevitable that the ideology of the existing order jettison the labor theory of value, and it is the necessity of doing so that largely explains both the "discovery" of a "new" theory of value and its rapid sweep to acceptance.

The labor theory of value had long since been outmoded by the Industrial Revolution and the substitution of machines for men as the source of wealth. By the middle of the nineteenth century it was obvious that large capital investment in machine processes was the way to wealth for both the individual and the economy as a whole and that human labor was but one factor of production, not the sole source of wealth. By 1850 common sense could no longer confirm the validity of a labor theory of value. Nevertheless, the theory hung on because of the ideological uses to which it could be put in justifying private property. When Marx turned the theory around and used it to attack property rights, the whole concept had to go.

Viewed in this light, the development of the new economics of 1870 must give us pause. It suggests that ideas are not accepted because they are "right" and rejected because they are "wrong" but that they are accepted when they are useful and rejected when their usefulness ends. In this case, the labor theory of value was part of the accepted canon of economic ideas as long as it could be used as part of the ideology of capitalism. When Marx destroyed its usefulness, the theory was discarded and replaced by the theory of marginal utility, which could support the theory of free markets and be used to belabor the Marxists.

Indeed, the new theory made refutation of Marx unnecessary, for it enabled the theory of private-enterprise capitalism to be rebuilt on a new basis. As the Austrian economist Eugen Böhm-Bawerk (1851–1914) pointed out in 1884, the entire Marxian analysis became irrelevant. This disciple of Karl Menger spent much of his career attacking Marxism in great detail, but he always felt that the best single argument was that the labor theory of value was just plain wrong. In England, Philip Wicksteed (1844–1927) came to the same conclusion at about the same time; he wrote that the entire Marxian analysis was invalid because it was based on labor instead of utility. The concensus of orthodox economists of the late nineteenth and early twentieth centuries was perhaps most succinctly stated by another Austrian, Friedrich von Weiser (1851–1926), who rejected the Marxian theory of surplus value as follows:

> This argument is not conclusive, if for no other reason than simply because it takes the ground of the labor-theory, which cannot be maintained for the developed conditions of national economy.

The ideology of capitalism had survived its first great crisis and had been reconstructed on new grounds.

SCIENTIFIC ADVANCES

Just as neoclassical economics had important ideological implications, it also served to make economics more scientific. This apparent paradox was due in part to the growth of academic interest in economics, reflected by a large increase in the number of economists teaching in universities, and in part to a growing interest in the scientific study of the social sciences as a whole. In the last half of the nineteenth century sociology emerged as a separate academic discipline, the first psychological laboratories were established, and the philosophy departments of major universities were beginning to spawn departments of economics and political science. The study of society was becoming more empirical, experimental, and systematic, and laws of social change and development were being explored by an increasingly large number of scholars.

Economics, of course, had always had a scientific cast, based on the theories of equilibrium pioneered by Adam Smith and the classical economists. This approach was greatly stimulated by the reformulation developed by the neoclassical economists. The foundations of the subject were reduced to the desires and wants of the individual, and the whole theoretical explanation of production, distribution, and prices was based on the single assumption of rational, individual self-interest.

One of the great driving forces in the growth of scientific thought is the effort to reduce complex explanations to simple ones, to find single laws for phenomena formerly explained by several. In this respect neoclassical economics was a major step forward in the growth of economics as a science, for instead of basing the theory of value on one set of ideas and the theory of distribution on three different explanations of the returns to the factors of production, all were based on marginalism.

Contributing further to the advancement of the subject was use of mathematical techniques of analysis and exposition. Concern with changes at the margin led inevitably to use of the calculus, for that mathematical technique had been specially developed to handle problems involving small quantitative increases and decreases. For example, the theory of marginal productivity could be conclusively proven, even under assumptions of perfect competition, only with the aid of a theorem from the calculus. The new trend was symbolized, perhaps, by the title of a book by Irving Fisher, a well-known American neoclassical economist, *Mathematical Investigations Into the Theory of Price.*

The development of symbolic logic also helped make economics more scientific, especially since it used the notational symbols of mathematicians. Walras' great book, in which he propounded the interrelatedness of all aspects of the economy based on rational consumer decisions, was largely an exercise in symbolic logic. One must be something of a mathematician to understand it and something of a theorist to appreciate it.

Even the critics of neoclassical economics contributed to the growing emphasis on the scientific approach. In Germany a group of "historical" economists criticized the lack of empirical verification and the excessive amount of theorizing that went into neoclassical economics and stressed the need for facts, facts, and more facts before valid generalizations could be made. In the United States a group of "institutional" economists made similar complaints, arguing that the structure and functioning of economic institutions must be fully understood before justifiable theoretical conclusions could be reached. Although orthodox neoclassical economists never gave up their basically deductive method of drawing conclusions from assumptions and premises — with a growing use of mathematical techniques — theories and conclusions were increasingly checked against facts, statistics, and experience. Theories without facts and facts without theories gave way to a blending of theoretical and empirical studies that remains the style of economics today.

8

The Family of Man

With the emergence of Marxism, the great debate over the economic system centered around the issue of socialism versus capitalism. The orthodox response based on the extremes of Darwinian individualism and the moderation of neoclassical economics served to further divide the antagonists. But the pattern of social thought is never simple. There are more than two or three possible responses in any ideological debate, and the issue of the proper organization of economic life brought forth a wide variety of ideas that opened up other dimensions of the problem. It was not just a question of socialized property and planning at one end of the scale versus private property and competitive enterprise at the other, with a variety of compromises forming a continuum between the two extremes. Other approaches, other formulations of the issue, and other solutions were offered.

One great middle ground involved the human side of man and his needs as a social being. Marx had looked on the social system as being divided into antagonistic social classes, with social conflict as the source of change. Orthodox economists, on the other hand, saw society as a mass of individual units brought into an uneasy equilibrium by the forces of the market. Yet a third group of economic thinkers considered man and society as a single interrelated unit, with the individual motivated by self-interest, by feelings of brotherhood, by curiosity, by ethical values, by his social and economic status. This complex view of the nature of man and society was developed in a wide variety of ways by different writers who, as a group, advocated a society in which human welfare was consciously sought as the chief objective of social policy. These men were the architects of the philosophy of the welfare state. Pragmatic yet visionary, critical yet hopeful, they built many of the ideas on which the mixed economies of Western Europe and North America are based. Their influence on contemporary public policy has far exceeded that of the socialists or the orthodox neoclassical economists.

PAPAL ECONOMICS

Pope Leo XIII (1810–1903) tried to find, in the abstract principles of social justice, a middle ground between the warring factions of capital and labor. In a famous encyclical of 1891 he defined the social problems of the age as essentially moral rather than economic and called for their solution on the basis of justice animated by charity. It was not a solution that could be measured by benefits and costs in the marketplace, and it was by no means "practical," but that was the whole point: morality and justice are not market phenomena but stand above the worldly considerations of profit and loss, wages and costs. Leo XIII called for consideration of economic issues in an entirely new dimension.

The Pope, who was born Gioacchino Vincenzo Pecci, had devoted his entire life to the service of the Roman Catholic Church. He was educated as a Jesuit, became a priest in 1837, and held a variety of administrative posts in the papal government, rising rapidly to become an archbishop in 1846 and a cardinal in 1853. He was elected Pope in 1878, at a time when the nationalism of the nineteenth century was causing severe problems for the relationship between Church and state in every European country and when industrialization was creating new social classes whose relationship to the Church was not yet clearly defined. Leo XIII held the papacy for a quarter of a century, and it was in large part through his efforts that the Catholic Church adapted itself to the new political and economic order.

In a series of encyclicals issued between 1878 and 1901, Leo XIII sought to analyze the problems of modern society and their remedies, the nature of the state and its relationship to the individual and the Church, and the fundamental economic problems of the age. One of his first encyclicals condemned socialism and upheld the right of private property, continuing a traditional position of the Church. But by 1891 he was prepared to take a much more advanced position. Problems of Church and state had largely been settled by compromise

in France, Germany, Belgium, Switzerland, and Austria-Hungary, so
that attention could be given to the struggle between capital and labor,
between capitalist and socialist, that was threatening to tear apart the
fabric of the European social order. In *Rerum Novarum*, sometimes
called *On the Condition of Labor*, he argued that "a remedy must be
found . . . for the misery and wretchedness which press so heavily at
this moment on the large majority of the very poor." He continued
with an indictment of laissez-faire policies:

> Working men have been given over, isolated and defenseless,
> to the callousness of employers and the greed of unrestrained
> competition. The evil has been increased by rapacious
> usury . . . still practiced by avaricious and grasping men. And to
> this must be added the custom of working by contract, and the
> concentration of so many branches of trade in the hands of a few
> individuals, so that a small number of very rich men have been
> able to lay upon the masses of the poor a yoke little better than
> slavery itself.

This passage, hardly distinguishable from the writings of avowed
socialists, was followed, however, by a condemnation of socialism and a
plea for private property as a natural right of the individual.

Leo XIII viewed the proper form of society as one in which the
interests of the community as a whole transcended those of the individual and in which economic relationships were motivated by good will,
brotherhood, and concern for the interests of others rather than by
pure profit-seeking acquisitiveness. Building on Catholic social
thought that went back to Thomas Aquinas in the thirteenth century
and beyond, Leo XIII saw larger community interests at stake than
merely those of the market. He criticized the rugged individualism of
the market economy and called for a return to human and community
values.

In placing the interests of the community above those of the
marketplace, Leo XIII assigned an important function to the state: it
ought to intervene in economic affairs whenever the welfare and preservation of society as a whole might be endangered, but always with
justice and fairness. It was quite proper for the state to limit hours of
work, establish minimum wages, prohibit child labor, and provide
other welfare legislation wherever required for the protection of
society and its members. Labor unions were also proper, so long as
they did not restrict membership and pursue selfish goals. Indeed,
Leo XIII argued for the organization of a Catholic labor union to
assure that the labor movement gave proper consideration to ethical
values. Viewed from the second half of the twentieth century, these
papal pronouncements seem mild indeed, but at the turn of the

century they were not, especially as they came from the leader of a religion which then and now has generally supported conservatism in political and economic affairs.

The tradition of Leo XIII has been continued by later popes, by the Catholic trade union movement, and by liberal theologians in the Church. Pope Pius XI commemorated the fortieth anniversary of *Rerum Novarum* in 1931 with another encyclical, *Quadragessimo Anno (Reconstructing the Social Order)*, which applied the same principles to problems of the depression and the rise of Fascism and Communism in Europe. It tried to find a middle ground between those warring factions in a humanitarian concern for human welfare that rejected the philosophy of laissez faire as well. In 1961 Pope John XXIII issued *Mater et Magistra (Christianity and Social Progress)* to restate the idea that man and community were one and to emphasize that both individual freedoms and individual welfare had to be reconciled in a society which stressed community values and social justice. Although these ideas have not been translated into specific economic policies or reforms anywhere in the world, they have helped to create a climate of opinion that gives high priority to equity in economic life.

PHILOSOPHERS OF THE WELFARE STATE

In England John A. Hobson, the Fabian socialists, and Richard H. Tawney led the fight for a positive liberalism designed to cure the social ills of an industrial society. They defined government's role as one that fosters those social relationships and institutions that enable man to be himself at his best. The state should remove hindrances to the good life and promote conditions that enable the individual to do and enjoy the things worth doing and enjoying.

Under the influence of these ideas England witnessed a quarter century of reform, including legislation for factory safety (1891, 1895), limited working hours for women and children (1895), the beginnings of slum clearance (1890), widened powers for labor unions (1890–1900), workmen's compensation and child-welfare legislation (1906), old-age pensions (1908), the beginnings of town planning and redevelopment (1909), and disability and sickness insurance (1911). The major components of the modern welfare state were being brought together.

John A. Hobson (1858–1940) was one of the chief exponents of the ideas behind this social legislation. He was denied a university post because of his unorthodox views, but from his pen flowed an unending stream of books and articles that shamed his orthodox contemporaries by their insight and criticisms. An early work, *The Physiology of Industry,* analyzed the causes of depressions and found them in inadequate consumer spending. *The Evolution of Modern Capitalism* criticized the industrial order for its monopoly, unequal income distribution, and depressions. *Imperialism* attacked the selfish expansion of the European states; its argument was later incorporated by Lenin into the Communist ideology. *Incentives in the New Industrial Order* proclaimed that socialism could work because it would utilize a broad spectrum of motivations, not just those of big business capitalism. *Work and Wealth*, however, was Hobson's most important work. In it he argued for a concept of the good life in which government would be responsible for a more equitable distribution of income and for social controls to ensure full employment and high wages and to promote health, education, and recreation. Hobson believed that government action could end poverty, unemployment, and insecurity and establish a society in which human happiness would prevail. Utopian, yes — but this was the vision that lay behind English social legislation. Hobson did not originate it, but he was its best spokesman.

— Hobson's ideals were similar to those of the Fabian Society, organized in 1883 by a group of English intellectuals whose ambitious goal was "reorganizing society in accordance with the highest moral possibilities" through a democratic socialist regime designed to promote "the greatest happiness of the greatest number." It was a small but very influential group; among the early members were the dramatist George Bernard Shaw, Sidney Webb, Graham Wallas, and Annie Besant, and they were joined later by the novelist H. G. Wells and by Beatrice Webb. The *Fabian Essays*, published in 1889 under Shaw's editorial leadership, advocated a gradual extension of state intervention in economic affairs to improve working conditions, replace monopoly with government ownership, and promote a more equalitarian distribution of income.

The society was named after the Roman general Fabius Maximus, "the delayer," who fought Hannibal, the Carthaginian commander, with what would now be called guerrilla tactics as opposed to full-scale battles. The name signified the society's political philosophy and plan of action. In opposition to the Marxists, the Fabians viewed the state not as an instrument of class warfare that had to be destroyed but as a means of social control that should be captured and used to promote social welfare. To this end they advocated formation of a labor party with a socialist program and were among the group that did successfully form such a party in 1906. They also sought to use local governments, which had been greatly strengthened by legislation of the late 1880's and early 1890's, to achieve their goals. The tactics of the Fabians, then, involved political action within the framework of democratic, parliamentary government. They worked to institute their reforms by convincing the general public of the correctness of their views and by publicizing their stand in a series of research reports and popular pamphlets.

The Fabian band enjoyed considerable success. Their work helped push the welfare legislation of pre-1914 England through Parliament, and they helped organize the Labour party. Although they failed in their attempts to use local governments for social reform and to establish government ownership of large-scale industries (coal, steel, electric power, finance, and railroads), their ideas and tactics lived on in the Labour party and came to fruition after World War II, when the society itself had a resurgence of activity and influence. Much of contemporary English welfare legislation and the socialization of transport, coal mining, and other basic industries can be traced back to the influence of the Fabians.

A different sort of influence was wielded by Richard H. Tawney (1880-1963), a scholar whose field of research was English economic history of the sixteenth century—a period considerably removed from the hurly-burly of political and economic issues of the twentieth century. But Tawney was a man of both ages. His masterly treatise on *The Agrarian Problem in the 16th Century* (1912) broke new ground in historical theory by analyzing the breakdown of the old agricultural, feudal order and the emergence of the modern market economy and society. Then, looking at modern society with the eyes of both an outraged reformer and an objective scholar, Tawney wrote three of the most important books of his time.

First came *The Acquisitive Society* (1920), where Tawney compared the functional society of the Middle Ages, in which each individual had his place, his duties, and his rewards, with the modern industrial world, in which productive effort gains little reward while the promoter, speculator, and *rentier* collect large sums of unearned income. Modern society should be reorganized, argued Tawney, so that rewards are received by those who expend work and effort, by those who perform the tasks that society needs if it is to function for the welfare of all. "It is foolish to maintain property rights for which no service is performed," said Tawney, "for payment without service is waste." Society, he argued, should be reformed along the functional lines of a socialist society.

Then came the most influential of all of Tawney's works, *Religion and the Rise of Capitalism* (1926). Going back to his academic field of the sixteenth century, Tawney took up the scholarly debate begun by the Germans Werner Sombart and Max Weber over whether the Protestant Reformation created the intellectual climate that made possible the rise of modern capitalism. Tawney agreed that the two were related, and that each influenced the other, but the major thrust of his argument was that the business activities of modern society were completely amoral. Ever since the Protestant ethic of hard work and worldly success had become ends in themselves, without reference to broader or higher values, business had been carried on without moral principles. It was almost as if modern man were continually re-enacting the Faust legend, selling his soul for material prosperity while relegating ethical values to a quickly forgotten two hours on Sunday. Tawney described the modern world as "the smiling illusion of progress won from the mastery of the material environment by a race too selfish and superficial to determine the purpose to which its triumphs shall be applied."

This plea for values going beyond material wealth was followed by *Equality* (1931), which argued persuasively for a society that would provide an equalitarian distribution of wealth through "the pooling of surplus resources by means of taxation, and the use of the funds thus obtained to make accessible to all, irrespective of their income, occupation or social position, the conditions of civilization which, in the absence of such measures, can be enjoyed only by the rich." Such equalitarianism would, in turn, support and sustain the democratic political framework that made it possible.

Tawney was an interesting man. The foremost historical scholar in an obscure and often uninteresting field, he used his detailed knowledge of the subject to cast new light on his own times. He developed a broad-ranging philosophy that raised basic criticisms of the economic life of his era. Tawney's solutions to the problems he described were socialistic because he believed that only through socialism could human values receive proper development.

VEBLEN, COMMONS, AND THE NEW DEAL

The philosophy of the democratic welfare state developed in the United States on much more pragmatic grounds than in England. There were no economic philosophers like Hobson and Tawney and no group of intellectual activists like the Fabians. The American approach developed through the work of a small group of economists who investigated the economic problems of business cycles, labor relations, monopoly and big business, and social welfare, and through political leaders from the progressive era to the New Deal. The basic theme of both groups was that modern industrial society faced serious problems that would not solve themselves and that the powers of government should be used to protect both the social fabric and the individuals within it from the often destructive forces of the market. The Americans sought workable solutions to specific problems within the traditional framework of American society, in contrast to the socialist philosophy that prevailed in England.

If any one writer were to be singled out as the most influential exponent of the philosophy underlying the American development, it would be Thorstein Veblen (1857–1929). Coming out of the rural Midwestern society that produced the Populist movement and William

Jennings Bryan, this son of a Norwegian immigrant studied philosophy at Johns Hopkins and Yale and economics at Cornell. He made a career out of failure, never rising above the rank of assistant professor in a teaching career at Chicago, Stanford, and Missouri. Even when he lectured at the New School for Social Research in New York City during the early twenties, his salary was paid in part by contributions from his former students. But Veblen's books made him famous, and his ideas earned him the respect of his fellow economists. He was elected to the presidency of the American Economic Association in 1924, but declined the honor with the comment that the position was not offered when it might have done him some good professionally.

There are innumerable stories about Veblen. He left the University of Chicago in 1906 under a cloud created partly by his unorthodox ideas and partly by his having taken a trans-Atlantic trip with a prominent Chicago woman — professors were not supposed to do such things. Although he was married, his escapades with women continued during his three years at Stanford, and the administration and several faculty members are said to have heaved great sighs of relief when he left. Apparently Veblen attracted the opposite sex: he is reported to have remarked about one coed, "What can you do when she moves in with you?" His wife didn't like it.

Veblen did not enjoy teaching. When he went to the University of Missouri in 1911, his reputation as an economist preceded him. Students flocked to register for his classes, but they were met by a man who mumbled into his beard and who, on the first day of classes, filled the blackboards with a long list of readings on which they were to be examined in a week. This brought the class down to manageable size — about a dozen students. Moreover, Veblen did not give grades above "C," in order to discourage those hoping to be selected for Phi Beta Kappa.

Veblen shone in his books. In *The Theory of the Leisure Class* (1899), one of the most influential books of the last hundred years, Veblen criticized the materialistic criteria of success in a pecuniary culture. Since the survival of an individual and his family depended on income, money and wealth became the standard by which all actions were judged. The wealthy spent their money conspicuously to prove their claims to success, and those with lesser incomes emulated the wealthy and their way of life: if the boss took a month-long vacation in Bermuda on his yacht, his secretary scrimped for years to take a one-week cruise to the Caribbean. Since leisure time was the greatest indication of success — showing that one did not have to work at all — the wealthy had many servants, did not allow their wives or children to work, and spent their time seeking pleasure. "Conspicuous leisure," "conspicuous consumption," and "pecuniary emulation" were inherent in the market economy, and all led to a vast waste of resources, productive effort, and time. Veblen did not state his views as to what alternative value systems might be desirable, but he clearly rejected those of the pecuniary culture.

Veblen's next book, *The Theory of Business Enterprise* (1904), carried the argument further. Here he distinguished between production for use and production for profit, pointing out that businessmen often prevented achievement of the former by pursuing the latter. The drive for profit led to restriction of output through monopoly. It held back technological advances, as business firms sought to protect their existing capital investment. It led to depressions and cutbacks in production, because of excessive extensions of credit and financial manipulations. It promoted separation of ownership and control in business, as efforts were made to control greater amounts of wealth with existing capital. It led to military expenditures and war through business control of political power. The single-minded pursuit of profit, in other words, prevented full realization of the gains that could be achieved by machine technology. Just as consumer attitudes led to waste in a pecuniary society, so also did the basic patterns of business behavior.

These two books, and Veblen's other writings, focused as much on economic and social change as they did on descriptions of the pecuniary society. The business and leisure classes might dominate a society, said Veblen, but change was inevitable. Technology had a life of its own, and scientists, engineers, and others were continually seeking better methods of production and more efficient systems of organization, irrespective of profits. On the other hand, businessmen and owners of wealth were "vested interests" who resisted change because it might upset their comfortable positions. A great conflict was therefore inherent between the march of technology and the conservatism of the existing order, between the interests of the community at large and those of the wealthy powers-that-be. A cultural lag inevitably must develop between the needs of society created by changing conditions and the established institutions supported by the leisure-class elite. Veblen saw this conflict polarizing around the two extremes of a technologically dominated socialism devoted to community welfare and useful production, on the one hand, and a military authoritarianism designed to protect the existing structure of power and wealth, on the other. He had predicted the rise of fascism as early as 1904.

Even though Veblen's conclusions might be doubted, his viewpoint could not be ignored: fundamental forces of change were at work, he argued, requiring adaptations in social, economic, and political institutions that would inevitably be opposed by those who had achieved wealth and success. Veblen may not have originated his point of view, but he gave it a solid theoretical foundation in his concepts of the relation between change and the vested interests.

Allied with his critique of the pecuniary society and the business system, these concepts gave direction as well as viewpoint to the movement for economic and social reform.

Veblen's influence was widespread. His pupils and followers investigated in detail the issues he emphasized. Wesley Mitchell studied business cycles and founded the National Bureau for Economic Research. Adolf Berle and Gardner Means wrote on the separation of ownership and control in the large corporation. Means and Walton Hamilton analyzed the pricing policies of big business. Leonard Ayres looked at the impact of changing technology on economic institutions. Robert and Helen Lynd studied the structure of community power in books like *Middletown* and *Middletown in Transition*, and C. Wright Mills did the same on a national scale in *The Power Elite*. Even literary criticism was affected; for example, Vernon Parrington applied Veblenian ideas in his monumental *Main Currents in American Thought*.

Paralleling Veblen's work and influence was that of John R. Commons (1862-1945). Where Veblen had articulated the basic approach and viewpoint of the twentieth-century reform movement, Commons and his followers pioneered specific measures and legislation. Commons was also a Midwesterner and he also studied at Johns Hopkins University in the 1880's, when it was the foremost American graduate school. His teaching career took him first to Wesleyan, then to Oberlin, Indiana, and Syracuse. While at Syracuse he published a study which argued that the growth of the state paralleled the development of the institution of private property, as society sought to control the economic power that accompanied accumulation of property. Such ideas, plus Commons' desire to add to the curriculum a course in labor problems, impelled the university administration to abolish his position. For the next four years, he worked with the United States Industrial Commission studying labor unions and labor-management relations and with the National Civic Federation promoting conciliation between labor and management.

In 1904 Commons returned to academia with a position at the University of Wisconsin, at the invitation of his old professor at Johns Hopkins, Richard T. Ely. He spent almost as much time on leave from the university to serve on government commissions as he did on the campus. His major interests were public utility regulation and labor problems. He helped draft Wisconsin's public utility law of 1907 and wrote extensively in favor of workmen's compensation, unemployment insurance, and peaceful collective bargaining. In 1911 he helped set up the Wisconsin Industrial Commission, which sought to develop mediation and conciliation in labor disputes. In 1914 he served on a similar national commission in Washington and in 1915 wrote a report calling for a national labor board to promote settlement of labor disputes through collective bargaining. He then turned to unemployment insurance and began the movement that led to enactment of such a law in Wisconsin in 1932 and nationally a few years later. Realizing that unemployment insurance could not work effectively without economic stabilization, Commons entered that area and in the 1920's became president of the National Monetary Association, which sought programs to achieve stability of credit and prices.

All these programs and policies later became major parts of the public economy of the United States: public utility regulation as part of a regulatory system for businesses "affected with the public interest"; collective bargaining and mediation to settle disputes between labor and management on a voluntary basis; promotion of economic stability at high levels of output and employment; and social legislation (unemployment insurance, workmen's compensation, and old-age insurance) to mitigate the chief harmful effects of the industrial system. Much of the New Deal legislation of the 1930's lay within the framework pioneered by Commons.

Underlying Commons' ideas was a philosophy of government that placed the state in the role of mediator between conflicting economic interests and between economic forces and the individual. Commons and other liberal reformers saw conflicts of interest, which had to be resolved with fairness to both sides, between business and the public, between labor and management, and, in broader terms, between the free operation of market forces and individual welfare. This view of conflict differed sharply from those maintained by the other two chief ideological positions—from that of the neoclassical economists, who saw harmony emerging in all areas out of the equilibrating forces of the market, and from that of the Marxists, who argued that class conflict would inevitably tear the social order apart. Commons accepted both of these concepts but went beyond them; he argued that market forces could reconcile some but not all of the conflicting interests of the modern world and that a complex industrial society continually created new conflicts whose equitable resolution required government action.

The reforming, social welfare philosophy expressed by Veblen and the policies pioneered by Commons and his associates came to fruition during the 1930's under the New Deal administrations of Franklin D. Roosevelt, when the concept of the welfare state became dominant. It is true that old ideas began to change before the thirties: witness the welfare legislation of New York and Wisconsin, the conservation movement prior to World War I, and the gradual acceptance by government of the use of monetary policy to promote economic stability. Crusaders and critics from the Populists onward had been forging the social philosophy of the New Deal. But the years from 1929 to 1933 were a great watershed in American social thought, and the legislation of the five years after 1933 created the framework within which the American economy continues to function more than a quarter of a century later.

The most important aspect of the New Deal philosophy was the belief that society as a whole, functioning through government, must protect itself and its members against the disruptive forces inherent in an industrial, market-oriented economy. This represented a great shift away from the philosophy that the self-adjusting market should be given free sway and that people, resources, and wealth should be treated essentially as commodites.

The New Deal administration practiced three main types of direct intervention in economic affairs to achieve its goals. First was its assumption of responsibility for approaching full employment prosperity as nearly as possible, although the Great Depression's unemployment was not conquered until World War II. The most effective method developed by the New Deal was to use the federal budget to assure an adequate level of total spending, and the budget deficits of the thirties were incurred in an effort to supplement inadequate private spending with public investment. There is little disapproval of this sort of policy today; it has been embodied in the Employment Act of 1946 and institutionalized in the President's Council of Economic Advisers. Both major political parties agree that responsibility for economic stability and expansion rests on the federal government.

A less successful form of intervention was embodied in the National Recovery Administration (NRA), the great effort to promote economic stability through cooperation between businessmen and labor in individual industries. The experiment failed and has been one of the most heavily criticized of the New Deal programs. The New Deal itself abandoned it and in the later thirties turned full circle to the policy of promoting competition as recommended by the Temporary National Economic Committee. Whatever the merits of the case, the spirit of the NRA lives on in two natural resource industries—petroleum and coal—although its philosophy is no longer part of the liberal creed. In the petroleum industry, the states regulate oil production, while the federal government supervises imports and acts to constrain oligopoly and quasi-cartelization abroad. The coal industry is today characterized by a high degree of labor-management cooperation and coordination. The fostering of free collective bargaining as a means of settling labor-management disputes became a national policy, and the National Labor Relations (Wagner) Act (1935) was passed to move in that direction.

The third main type of government intervention in economic affairs was regional land-use planning based on water resources. Typified by the Tennessee Valley Authority, the principle of such planning was the outgrowth of a number of pre-New Deal policies —reclamation, waterway development, forest conservation, city planning, and the controversy over electric power development. Today we take for granted the desirability of unified development of water resources and related land uses. Debate over various programs is limited to the respective roles of the federal and state governments and private enterprise.

Supplementing the New Deal's economic interventionism was a new view of the individual's place in society. The older proposition —that the individual seeking his own best interests would contribute most to society as a whole, and the corollary that the unsuccessful ought to bear the cost burden themselves—was not tenable in an industrial society, particularly one plagued by a depression that crushed even intelligent, hard-working businessmen. In its place arose the belief that society had a responsibility for the welfare of each person, partly because the individual contributed to society by work-ing, by raising a family, and by participating generally in the activities of the social order, and partly because the problems of a complex society were often too great to be solved by the individual. The posi-tion was given support by the belief that the individual functions more effectively, both in his own interest and as a contributor to society, in a secure environment. Another goal of New Deal policy was therefore to create sufficient economic security to release greater individual ener-gies that would, in the long run, more than compensate for the costs involved. In practice this meant the passage of a range of welfare measures—unemployment insurance, social security, workmen's compensation, and federal grants-in-aid in health and education —which also have achieved general acceptance today.

Another major tenet of New Deal social philosophy was that businessmen had social responsibilities beyond mere profit-making. In the pre-New Deal era, profit and success were their own justification; wealth reflected not only hard work and ability but also the fact that the search for wealth resulted in meeting the needs of others, "as if by an invisible hand." By contrast, the New Deal stressed that the market economy often ran roughshod over human and social values and that individual gain was not always synonymous with social good. Success and profit were not enough; business had to justify itself on other grounds. Nowhere was this requirement spelled out in detail, but New Deal legislation implied that it included reasonably stable operations, broadly effective labor-management relations, reasonable prices, and straightforward financial activities.

It has sometimes been said that the antagonism of business toward the New Deal resulted from the lesser place in society given business by the rise of government intervention, compounded by the business-man's view of federal aid to labor unions as a challenge to himself within his own enterprise. There may be truth in the argument, but perhaps even more significant was the challenge to business as an end in itself. In effect, the New Dealer said to the businessman, "You're a success, but look at the mess you've made of the economy and how much it has cost in human suffering." Such a viewpoint—assuming that the businessman bore sole responsibility for the "mess"—is hardly calculated to make friends.

It is important to note that the New Deal leaders did not fight their political battles on philosophical grounds but rather by promoting legislation that embodied bits and pieces of an applied program of action. Too pragmatic for ideological battles, and much too shrewd a politician for abstract argument, Franklin D. Roosevelt led the New Deal toward specific goals and specific legislation. When he did try to uphold his program on an ideological basis—in the 1937 battle over reorganization of the Supreme Court—he was badly beaten, although ultimately he won approval of his social legislation proposals. Roosevelt's emphasis on practical action rather than theoretical debate was politically sound, and it was thoroughly within the American tradition. More important, it minimized the dissension, class conflict, and ideological warfare inevitably engendered by the rise to predominance of a new social philosophy.

Especially helpful in reducing the bitterness that did result was preservation of the individual's right to spend or save as he pleased, to choose his occupation, and to make his own business decisions. Although the New Deal restructured much of the country's social and economic framework, its methods never included detailed planning or controls nor did it encroach upon personal decision-making—one of the basic tenets of American individualism.

It is unlikely that there will be any significant reduction of the government's role in social security programs, of its insistence upon free collective bargaining as the nation's labor policy, of its promotion of coordinated development programs for water resources, whether such programs are privately or publicly managed, or of its use of federal monetary and fiscal policies to promote both economic growth and full employment. The economic philosophy of the New Deal is still the basis of national policy in the United States and underlies the "Great Society" of the 1960's. It has been extended into new fields of social legislation, and it remains controversial, but the more important government programs are generally accepted as beneficial to both the individual and the nation as a whole.

9

The Keynesian Revolution

In 1936 the whole direction and emphasis of modern economics was transformed by the appearance of a single book. Its forbidding title was *The General Theory of Employment, Interest, and Money,* and it was written by the most controversial English economist of the time, John Maynard Keynes. It dealt with crucial problems of employment and unemployment at a time when the world economy was in the grip of the most disastrous and widespread depression it had ever experienced. Although many people had given up hope of ever rebuilding worldwide prosperity and a viable economic system, this book offered a theoretical analysis diagnosing the patient as seriously ill but not beyond hope and prescribing remedies that could restore his health. Keynes and his suggested policies immediately became the center of controversy among professional economists and politicians. Although damned by left-wing radicals and right-wing conservatives alike, Keynesian economics nevertheless swept aside almost all opposition among economists to establish a new orthodoxy within the profession. Together with *The Wealth of Nations* and *Capital, The General Theory of Employment* stands as one of the key books in the development of economics.

JOHN MAYNARD KEYNES

The man responsible for this revolution in social thought occupied a unique position in English public life. A member of the social and intellectual elite that had come to dominate public affairs in England, his unorthodox criticism of accepted economic policies seemed to fly in the face of all that the reigning leaders believed. Keynes was a critic of the Establishment from within the Establishment itself.

Keynes was born in 1883 in Cambridge, England, the son of a prominent economist and logician, John Neville Keynes. He was educated at Eton and Cambridge, where he studied philosophy and economics. A favorite and brilliant pupil of Alfred Marshall, he absorbed the essentials of neoclassical economics and always accepted its analysis of production and distribution. His special field was monetary economics, and he worked with the government on problems of Indian finance, and at the Treasury, in addition to lecturing at Cambridge. During the years before World War I, he became a member of the Bloomsbury set of artists and writers, which included such intellectuals as Lytton Strachey, E. M. Forster, Virginia Woolf, and Roger Fry. Typical of this group's attitude were Strachey's biographies debunking *Eminent Victorians* — brilliant, critical, but generally accepting the sense and order of the existing social system. The attitude was also typical of Keynes: himself a product of a comfortable social class that considered itself born to rule because of its intelligence, training, and dedication, he nevertheless sought always to achieve better ways of doing things within the framework of the old verities. By all accounts, Keynes was a brilliant snob with a most engaging personality, but he also had an analytical mind that could immediately probe to the essentials of a problem, perceiving as well its broader ramifications and its connections with other issues. If there had to be an intellectual elite, it was fortunate that a man like Keynes was part of it.

Keynes had worked at the Treasury during World War I, making quite a name for himself as a financial expert, and in 1919 he was the Treasury's chief representative at the Versailles peace conference. With an intuitive understanding of world politics and a detailed knowledge of international finance, he knew that a stable peace depended on a magnanimous settlement and a realistic reparations burden for Germany. While statesmen argued over boundaries, frontiers, and national prestige, Keynes realized that the economic problems of Europe were more important than the political. When the peace treaty went the other way, demanding hugh reparations and ignoring economic realities, Keynes resigned and returned home to write a slashing attack on the peace settlement and the men who developed it. In one of the most prophetic works of the age, *The*

Economic Consequences of the Peace, he forecast the breakdown of the agreements and much of the economic turmoil that followed. The book was a sensation, but it largely destroyed Keynes' official contacts with government for a decade.

He went back to lecturing at Cambridge, became an executive of two insurance companies and several investment firms, speculated heavily in foreign exchange, stocks, and commodities to amass a substantial fortune, became active in the Liberal party, wrote extensively in *The Nation* and other journals, patronized art, music, and ballet, and married one of the great dancers of the Diaghilev Ballet.

He continued to criticize British economic policy, particularly the unwise effort to return to the gold standard in the mid-1920's, and from this controversy came his most important contribution to economics. Keynes attacked the policy primarily on the ground that its goal of achieving international economic stability was incorrect, that internal economic welfare was far more important. Stable prices and high levels of employment were more desirable than stability in the value of the pound on the foreign exchanges, he argued, pointing out that a return to the gold standard at the prewar exchange rate would seriously diminish British exports and cause domestic wages, prices, employment, and output to fall, just as they had a hundred years before, at the close of the Napoleonic wars, because of similar policies. Keynes advocated a managed monetary system in place of the automatism of the gold standard, but fiscal fundamentalism proved too strong, England went back to the gold standard, and disaster struck — unemployment, falling prices, and a nationwide general strike. Economic stagnation prevailed in England through the rest of the twenties, once again fulfilling Keynes' prophecy.

One reason no one listened to Keynes in 1923-1924 was that he had not developed a successful theoretical defense of his position. In order to demonstrate the deflationary effects of the government's monetary policy, he would have had to analyze the interconnections between the gold standard and the domestic level of employment and to prove that the orthodox economic analysis of those relationships, which applied Say's Law of Markets, was wrong. He was unable to do so at the time, but his keen mind saw that a thorough revision of the theory of employment and its relationship to monetary theory had to be developed. Keynes devoted the next twelve years to that task.

The first effort, a two-volume *Treatise on Money*, published in 1930 just after the stock market crash, did not do the job. In many ways Keynes' most scholarly book, it presented the basic framework of his new theory but left enough theoretical points unresolved to arouse more professional criticism than acceptance. Nevertheless, his point of view was important. The main argument of the book rested on the distinction between investment and savings and the different goals that motivated them. Say's Law insisted that the two had to be equal, but Keynes declared that they need not be. When savings exceeded investment, economic activity would decline; if the opposite were true, economic activity would increase. The remedies were those that Keynes had previously recommended—a managed monetary system to help maintain equality between savings and investment and hence to promote economic stability, supplemented by public works expenditures to mitigate the effects of whatever depression and unemployment should occur.

At the time the *Treatise* was published, both economists and government officials were unaware of the seriousness of the depression, public opinion had not yet realized the need for drastic remedies, and most people expected the market contraction to be short. Keynes, of course, did not share these views but returned to his writing to attempt a second frontal attack on the accepted economic ideas.

THE CLIMATE OF OPINION IN THE MID-1930'S

The product of this phase of Keynes' labor was *The General Theory of Unemployment, Interest, and Money.* This book made an immediate sensation, not because it proposed a theory radically different from that in the *Treatise* but because, by the time of its publication in 1936, a path had been prepared for it. First, Keynes' previous publications had familiarized economists and policy-makers with his general point of view. Second, several other important economists had also broken through the orthodoxy of Say's Law of Markets to arrive at related conclusions. And third, the climate of opinion had shifted, particularly during the early years of the Great Depression, toward greater acceptance of ideas that tied the level of prosperity to total spending.

One vitally important element of the later Keynesian analysis was developed by a Russian economist with strong Marxist leanings, Michel Tugan-Baranowsky (1865–1919), who, ironically enough, had studied at Vienna under Eugen Böhm-Bawerk, mentioned in Chapter Seven as the most vigorous anti-Marxist among the neoclassical economists but who today is the darling of the right-wing anti-Keynesians. Tugan-Baranowski argued that a regular flow of savings comes into capital markets from consumers with relatively fixed incomes; that the investment process is, by contrast, highly volatile; and that the resultant disparities between the flow of savings and the flow of investment are at the root of the business cycle. These disparities could not be overcome by changes in the rate of interest, he declared, because many people who saved were motivated by reasons other than the rate of return they earned.

A far more important breakthrough was made by an eccentric Swedish economist, Knut Wicksell (1851-1926), who once spent a term in jail for violating a law that prohibited public advocacy of birth control and planned parenthood. Nevertheless, Wicksell was a brilliant scholar whose work made it possible for the next generation of Swedish economists and for Keynes to develop the contemporary theory of national income.

According to the orthodox theory of full employment embodied in Say's Law of Markets, any money saved would find its way to investment through the money markets. If there were a tendency for savings to exceed investment, a decline in the rate of interest would quickly right matters; if investment were to outrun the supply of savings, the rate of interest would rise and re-establish equality. If this equality of savings and investment occurred at relatively high price and wage levels that left some labor unemployed, wages would fall —bringing the price level down with them—until all resources were productively employed.

Wicksell noticed, however, that the actual course of events did not substantiate the theory. On the contrary, when loans and investment were at low levels and hoarding of cash was widespread, interest rates were high and it was almost impossible to borrow; on the other hand, at the peak of a boom, when investment was high and cash balances were low, interest rates were also relatively low. This was, in fact, diametrically opposed to the theory, so Wicksell attempted a reconstruction of it. He postulated that there was a natural rate of interest consistent with full employment and with equality between savings and investment. However, the market rate of interest could differ from this natural rate for a variety of reasons, and when it did the economy would either expand or contract. The essential point was that the natural equilibrium was brought about not by changes in the rate of interest but by changes in the *level of economic activity*—that is, by increases or decreases in output and employment.

This was the great reformulation that ultimately led to the Keynesian revolution. Wicksell's concept of natural and market rates of interest was soon dropped, even by his brilliant followers among the Swedish economists, who included Gunnar Myrdal, Bertil Ohlin, and Dag Hammarskjöld, who later became a great Secretary General of the United Nations. But his fundamental concept of changes in the level of total spending as the equilibrating mechanism of the economy was retained and built into the economics of national income as we know it today.

Closer to Keynes than Wicksell was D. H. Robertson, one of Keynes' younger colleagues at Cambridge. In 1926 Robertson published a short book on the business cycle that stressed the importance of the relationship between savings and the demand for capital goods. The banks had a dual function, he pointed out, to provide the proper amount of working capital for business at the same time that they

opposition to the old theory that the rate of interest determined equality between savings and investment and that wage reductions would lead to full employment. In terms of the events of the 1930's and the climate of political opinion, the new theory was far more realistic than the old. Right or wrong, it at least offered some hope that proper policies could cure the ills of the economy, and it laid down the general lines that those policies should follow.

THE MEANING OF KEYNESIAN ECONOMICS

The *General Theory* was given a mixed reception. To judge by the reviews in scholarly journals, the older generation of economists missed its significance or did not understand its obviously intricate theoretical complexities. But younger economists seized upon it avidly, seeking both to fathom its difficulties and to spread its gospel. In particular, a group of young economists in the United States government used its ideas to justify the already existing policy of public works, deficit spending, and easy money. They were aided by two somewhat older men, Gerhard Colm, a German refugee then in the Bureau of the Budget whose experience in Germany had given him an understanding of the need for expansionary economic policies, and Alvin Hansen, a Harvard professor who became the chief American exponent of the Keynesian point of view. Hansen produced a voluminous series of works publicizing the new ideas, while Colm and others worked quietly and anonymously within the government to build effective policies. But conservatives, young and old, reacted with horror against the ideas that seemed to be destroying the verities of hard money, savings, and fiscal restraint; "Keynesian economics" came to be a term of opprobrium in their circles.

Keynes, meanwhile, was *hors de combat.* Illness and a heart attack temporarily retired him within a year after the publication of the *General Theory,* and by the time he recovered, the Second World War had begun. During the war Keynes acted as an advisor of the British Treasury and helped negotiate major loans from the United States. After the war he helped formulate the Bretton Woods plan for an International Monetary Fund to help stabilize the world economy and avoid some of the pitfalls of the twenties. Knighted for his efforts, he died in 1946 at the age of sixty-two, recognized for what he was, the greatest economist of his time, overshadowed—perhaps—only by Adam Smith among economists of all time.

Keynes had almost single-handedly developed the rationale for the basic economic policies of the second half of the twentieth century in the nations of Western Europe and North America. Those policies recognize the great advantages to be obtained from the self-adjusting market mechanism explained so clearly by the neoclassical economists.

The welfare-maximizing consumer and the profit-maximizing producer, meeting in the competitive marketplace, bring about a pattern of production that most closely matches the wants of consumers. By and large, the argument runs, the free economy can be relied upon to allocate resources to the best advantage, and it is assisted by maintaining competition and by setting up special means for resolving special conflicts. Although the level of economic activity—determined by total spending, saving, and investment—must be managed by government in the interest of the nation as a whole, the economy nevertheless can be left free to respond to the decisions of individual consumers and producers. The larger import of Keynesian economics is that individual freedom and social order are consistent with each other within the framework of prosperity for all.

Chapter

10

Economic Planning

While Keynes was leading the way toward new policies designed to preserve and revitalize the market economy, a new challenge was arising. During the 1920's and 1930's socialist leaders in the Soviet Union devised methods of large-scale economic planning which brought rapid rates of economic growth and transformed a backward, rural economy into an industrial giant. The costs of the program were high, but its basic goals were achieved.

Many western economists argued at first that a planned economy must fail, but others examined the theory of planning in greater detail — explored its rationale and its operating techniques — and concluded that an efficient system was quite feasible. A number of underdeveloped, formerly colonial nations experimented with considerable success with a range of socialist and quasi-socialist, planned and semi-planned economies. Thus, both theory and practice have shown that economic planning can work effectively, and the issue in recent years has been the compatibility of planning with economic and political freedom.

PLANNING IN THE SOVIET UNION

The conclusion that economic planning can work was not always as obvious as it appears today. In the years immediately after the Russian Revolution, from 1917 to 1921, it seemed that the economy of the new Soviet state would gradually grind to a halt. Revolution, counterrevolution, and war destroyed most of the industry that had not been lost to foreign countries as the result of the peace settlement in Eastern Europe. The new government was not prepared to manage factories, and the former owners could hardly be expected to operate in a regime dedicated to their elimination. The peasants had seized the large agricultural estates and ate most of the reduced output instead of marketing it to supply the cities. When the government sent soldiers to seize grain, a peasant revolt threatened. And with the old bureaucracy gone tax collection failed, the government resorted to printing presses to obtain money, and inflation further complicated the economic chaos that developed.

Drastic measures were called for. The government shifted to a "New Economic Policy" that represented a retreat from full nationalization of trade and industry; light industry and retail trade were returned to private enterprise, but the government retained the "commanding heights" of the economy—heavy industry, power, transportation, banking, and much wholesale trade. The economy responded well. Output rose to its prewar levels in most industries by 1928. Reconstruction was rapid, and the government gained valuable experience in planning the nationalized industries. The first great crisis was over.

But new problems were at hand. Russia was still the most backward country in Europe. Its peasant agriculture was primitive by modern standards, much of the population was illiterate, and a large part of its "industrial" production was carried on by handicraft methods. Yet here was a nation faithful to a Marxist ideology which postulated that socialism would naturally evolve in highly industrialized economies in which the working class comprised a majority of the population. Compounding the problem was the fact that world revolution had failed and fear that the U.S.S.R. might be attacked at any time by the antagonistic capitalist countries that surrounded it.

V. I. Lenin (1870-1924) had laid down the basic lines on which these problems could be resolved. He had led the Bolshevik revolution to a successful conclusion after convincing his followers that Russia could by-pass the capitalist industrial era and move directly from an agricultural, semi-feudal society into the socialist era. The instrument of transition was to be rapid and large-scale industrialization, building the working-class society in which socialism could flourish. During the transition an alliance between workers and peasants (but not the well-to-do peasants, the "kulaks") under a workers' dictatorship was necessary, but greatest priority had to be given to constructing an urban, industrial society. Lenin died before his strategy could be translated into specific policies, and a great public debate took place among Soviet economists and political leaders over methods of planning and rates of growth. Until it was ended by Stalinist authoritarianism in 1930, with the first of the purge trials, this debate produced some extremely revealing discussions of economic development policy.

One approach (called by Stalin the "right deviation") was advocated by the moderates, led by Nikolai Bukharin, the Communist party's leading Marxist theoretician. He had in 1920 co-authored a famous treatise on economics which announced that the economic laws of capitalism no longer applied to the new Soviet state, which therefore had tremendous freedom to experiment with planning and other policies. By the later twenties he had shifted his position, however, arguing that the nation's rate of economic growth was limited by the amount of agricultural surplus that could be produced to feed the cities and to export in exchange for machinery. Industry had to grow, but two of its chief tasks were production of agricultural machinery and of consumer goods for sale to the peasants as an inducement for them to market their products. Bukharin was concerned about the loyalty of the peasantry to the regime—and well he might be—and was willing to restrict industrial development to the level made possible by expansion of agricultural production on a voluntary basis. This policy was based on the belief that fundamental economic relationships —such as those between industry and agriculture, heavy industry and consumer goods—determined the possible level of economic development and that it was dangerous for planners to try to expand beyond the level inherent in those relationships. Bukharin also tied his policies to foreign affairs. World revolution had to be temporarily postponed, he argued, partly because the first attempt had not succeeded and partly because the regime had to build firm support at home to resist the unfriendly capitalist powers, which meant gaining the allegiance of the peasants by not pushing them too hard.

A second approach, opposing that of the moderates, was put forward by the "left wing" of the Communist party, led by Leon Trotsky (1879-1940), Lenin's right-hand man during the revolution. The chief economist of this faction was Evgeni Preobrazhenski, who had been co-author with Bukharin of the 1920 treatise but now opposed him. The development strategy proposed by this group was to press the economy to the utmost, to attain the maximum possible rate of industrialization at all costs, squeezing living standards in order to free resources for industrial development and using the power of the state to extract the maximum surplus from agriculture for food, raw materials, and export. Agriculture was to be transformed by mechanization and by the formation of large collective farms. The left wing scorned the balanced planning advocated by Bukharin in favor of deliberate economic distortion for rapid industrialization. Like Bukharin, they also related their policies to the international situation, arguing that the Soviet state could never be secure in a capitalist world; that the Soviet Union could best protect itself by fostering world revolution; and that the best way to foster revolution was to demonstrate the superior productivity of socialism through impressive economic growth, which would also hinder a capitalist attack by bringing the working classes of other nations to Russia's support.

The great industrialization debate clearly involved the gravest of issues for the U.S.S.R., and the wily Joseph Stalin (1879–1953) used it as a stepping-stone to full power. He took an intermediate position at first, supporting rapid industrialization and "taut" planning as advocated by the left but siding with the right against collectivization of agriculture, in order to conciliate the peasantry. On the issue of world revolution, also, he aligned himself with Bukharin and the right, and on the basis of this alliance was able to defeat Trotsky in a contest for power and drive him into exile. Then, in an amazing political turnabout, he suddenly advocated the left's agricultural policy, accelerated the rate of capital accumulation beyond even that faction's expectations, and used the support he thereby gained to purge Bukharin and his followers. The debate was thus resolved by the establishment of ambitious development goals and a method of economic planning to achieve them, with the Stalin dictatorship as a major driving force behind the whole system.

Stalin stated the U.S.S.R.'s basic goals in 1928. They included "the final victory of socialism in our country," "an adequate industrial base for defense," and economic growth "to overtake and outstrip the advanced capitalist countries." The goals were essentially political and ideological in nature, although economic means were to be used to achieve them. "Maximum capital investment in industry" to achieve a "fast rate of industrial development" was the path to be followed, said Stalin, and this required "a state of tension in our plans."

The planning technique in general was not complicated, although the development of administrative details required much experimentation. The desired expansion of the economy was determined by top government leaders, who selected targets which would press the economy to its limits. A few key industries such as coal, power, steel, and machinery were selected as "leading links" and given top priority. The rest of the economy was tied to the target industries by a system of "balanced estimates," which determined the inputs and outputs of all sectors of the economy needed to achieve the goals for the leading links and, through them, for the economy as a whole. Production plans for individual enterprises were calculated on the basis of these industry-wide balances and supplemented by corresponding plans for finance and labor.

The ambitious goals and taut planning required that strong incentives be developed to draw forth the best efforts of the Russian people. Here the Soviet growth strategy ran into difficulty, because restrictions on output of consumer goods held back any significant increase in living standards. Any effort to increase production of consumer goods meant that much less effort available for expansion of industry; every ton of steel used for refrigerators meant one ton of steel less for electrical generators; every man-hour spent for construction of housing meant one man-hour less for building a power dam. For a time this problem was avoided by reducing unemployment, drawing women into the labor force, and shifting workers from agriculture to industry. Some incentive was provided by raising wages and salaries periodically, but with production of consumer goods held down, increased wages only drove prices up, and the incentive effect was merely temporary. Widening the differences between wage rates for jobs of differing skills also helped, but this practice was limited by its inconsistency with the equalitarian principles of socialism and by the fact that it brought lower standards of living to lower-income groups, who could afford to buy only a small share of the limited quantity of consumer goods. "Socialist" incentives were also tried — honors, medals, publicity, and various special benefits awarded to workers who exceeded existing production norms. But, in the end, the regime was forced to use compulsory methods, however reluctant it may have been to do so. Political goals required political incentives.

This was particularly true in agriculture. The shift from individual farms to collectives in the early 1930's aroused sharp resistance from the peasants and was the major cause of the terrible famine of 1933. The system facilitated agricultural mechanization and substantially increased output, however, and it enabled the regime to apply planning to agriculture and to ensure that the entire increase in output went to the state rather than to the farmers. Compulsory deliveries of farm products at low prices were instituted, and restrictions were placed on the uses of private farm plots. But these measures gave little incentive to individual peasants to improve farming methods, and production stagnated after the initial increase in output.

Other compulsory and restrictive measures became necessary for industrial workers as well. Regulations designed to reduce labor mobility were introduced in the late 1930's and, when World War II began, were extended to prohibit a man's quitting his job without getting permission from the plant manager; legal penalties were imposed for tardiness, unexcused absence, consistent failure to fulfill work norms, and other economic "crimes." Perhaps justified under wartime conditions, these negative incentives for labor continued in force until the early 1950's.

The power of the state rather than economic incentive was used to assure plan fulfillment. The Stalinist system of authority became as much a part of Soviet economic development strategy as the industrialization drive and taut planning. At the same time, of course, the Stalinist concentration camps had appeared as part of the Soviet scene. Although their purposes were primarily political rather than economic, they further darkened the already gray picture.

The system couldn't continue indefinitely. After Stalin's death, his successors attempted to gain the support of the people by eliminating much of the repression and by producing more consumer goods to raise living standards. Inevitably, the rate of economic growth slowed down as the hard-driving Stalinist pattern of authority was eased. Agriculture remained stagnant and backward; after an initial increase in farm output in 1953-1958, obtained by opening huge areas of new land in central Asia and by providing greater incentives to the peasants, production levels stabilized rather than continuing to rise. Industrial expansion also began to level off, despite administrative reorganizations and other efforts to sustain its high rates of growth, and major inefficiencies in resource allocation became apparent. A new crisis in economic policy was at hand, marked by the fall of Khrushchev in 1964 and by another debate over economic goals and planning methods.

Two new ideas are brewing. One involves the use of computers and mathematical methods of analysis to increase the efficiency of the planning system, implying greater centralization. Far more important, however, are suggestions to more closely fit production of consumer goods to consumer wants by using the market mechanism. A group led by Professor Yevsei Liberman of the University of Kharkov advocates giving plant managers greater freedom to select methods of production and to produce the kinds of products demanded by consumers, while reducing the powers of higher planning personnel. Rewards and incentive would be based more heavily on enterprise profits than on fulfillment of specified output levels. These proposals, already tried on an experimental basis, were made the basis of major economic reforms announced in 1965 that imply a reduction in the authority of the central planners and that allow greater exercise of initiative at local levels.

The Soviet economy is entering a new phase in its economic development. More than a third of a century of rapid economic growth has made it the second industrial nation of the world. Significant increases in living standards have occurred. Its scientific achievements rank high. Tremendous advances have been made in health, welfare, and education. Yet the centralized planning appropriate in the earlier stages of economic development, when the chief task was to raise the rate of savings and investment and accomplish drastic structural change quickly, may not be appropriate as the complexity of the economy grows and efficient use of existing resources is increasingly important. In addition, changing techniques of production affect incentives. The former technology of coal, steel, and railroads required a labor force endowed mainly with muscle, and such workers were effectively managed by compulsory devices despite low incomes. This has been true of most industrial nations at that stage of development, but in most cases authority has been applied by business firms rather than by government. A technology of automation, computers, synthetic materials, and electric power, however, requires educated and trained personnel who must be motivated in other ways. The Stalinist strategy for economic growth may well have been quite suitable to its time, but new paths are being sought in an effort to continue Soviet economic development at a rapid pace.

THE THEORY OF PLANNING

While the Soviet Union was forging a practical system of planning based largely on political goals, economists in other countries debated whether or not planning as a purely economic system could be efficient. They had little experience with public ownership, they knew little about planned economies, and even the traditional socialist literature had little to say on the topic. Moreover, most orthodox economists were so imbued with the beauties of the theory of the self-adjusting private-enterprise economy that they tended to dismiss economic planning as impractical, and the early difficulties of the Soviet economy seemed to confirm these first impressions.

One of the leaders in the attack on planning was Ludwig von Mises, an Austrian neoclassical economist who argued that socialism and planning could not provide a rational basis for economic decision-making. Writing in 1920 at the height of the Soviet Union's early difficulties, he pointed out that public ownership of the means of production precluded the establishment of a market for capital. Without such a market there could be no price for capital, no rate of interest to express relative scarcities, and hence no rational basis for determining how much capital should be accumulated and how it should be used. These decisions could be made by planners, he said, but they would not be rational ones that used the resources of the nation efficiently.

Interestingly enough, Von Mises' argument had been refuted some years before by an Italian economist, Enrico Barone, who had maintained that accounting prices established by planners could substitute for prices set in competitive markets, at least in theory. However, followers of Von Mises continued the attack, dismissing Barone's theoretical solution as impractical because it would require literally millions of decisions based on a vast amount of information about consumer preferences which plainly was not available to any planning board. Even if the information were available, solutions would be obsolete by the time they were calculated — electronic computers were not known in the 1920's, of course.

This argument was answered by two economists who began from widely different viewpoints. One was a conservative American neo-classicist, Fred M. Taylor, whose presidential address to the American Economic Association in 1928 demonstrated that Barone's solution could be achieved by a trial-and-error process. Consumers could be left free to spend their incomes in any way they liked, according to Taylor, while planners simply established prices which cleared the markets — that is, which precluded shortages and gluts — and which equaled costs of production. Production decisions would be determined by the quantities that could be sold at those prices. Once a balance had been achieved, the planners could be reasonably sure that resources were being allocated rationally.

The second answer was published in 1936–1937 by the socialist Oscar Lange, a Polish economist who was to become an important participant in that country's planned economy after World War II. In a much more elaborate analysis than that presented by Taylor, he showed that a planning board could simulate the market process by a trial-and-error method of setting prices and establishing a profit-maximizing rule for decisions by individual plant managers. The result would be maximization of consumer welfare along the lines of the competitive private-enterprise economy. Furthermore, the restrictions of monopoly could be eliminated and full employment assured by planning the level of investment. To this the English economist Arthur Pigou added that the private-enterprise economy did not always work well, anyway, as attested by the disparity between its description in economic theory and its actual operation.

The arguments of Taylor and Lange carried the day. Few economists today will argue that planning per se must fail, or even that it must be inefficient, although many would say that excessively detailed central planning will not work effectively. There are obvious difficulties involved in planning, and its actual operation in a given country may be criticized, but the theoretical argument has been won by those who argued in favor of planning.

Critics, too, have shifted ground. Taking their cue from the European dictatorships of the 1930's, they now argue that planning may be workable in an economic sense, but only at the expense of personal and political freedom. The foremost statement of this position was made by Friedrich von Hayek, another Austrian economist, in *The Road to Serfdom* (1944). This little book argues that once government intervention in the free market begins it must inevitably lead to socialism and that socialist planning leads inevitably to loss of freedom. There is no stopping place along the path to oppression.

The development of planning in recent years does not support Hayek's contention, no matter how realistic it may have seemed in the last days of World War II. The Soviet Union itself has significantly eased the authoritarianism imposed by Stalin, and experiments have recently been made to rely more heavily on market forces in making economic decisions. Yugoslavian central planners have made a conscious effort to reduce their own power, develop management by the workers themselves, and rely heavily on the operation of markets in making price and production decisions. In France a system of "indicative," or "target," planning has been developed in which goals for economic growth are fostered primarily by financial inducements to private enterprise, government management of some important nationalized industries, and control over the financial system — leaving individual decision-making largely untouched. In the underdeveloped nations of the world, planning for growth takes place within many kinds of political frameworks. The great variety of social and political systems, with greater or lesser degrees of planning, indicates that no simple relationship exists between planning and authority and that a planned economy need not be modeled on that of the Soviet Union or the dictatorships of the 1930's.

PLANNING IN UNDERDEVELOPED NATIONS

The underdeveloped nations have experimented heavily with a variety of planning methods. They emerged from World War II either independent or on the verge of independence but backward in both living standards and economic development. Like the Soviet Union in the 1920's, they had to break the fetters of traditionalism and accelerate their rates of economic growth if they were ever to become a real part of the world economy.

These countries of Asia, Africa, and Latin America had been caught in a vicious circle of underdevelopment. Low productivity and low incomes meant that savings were inadequate to achieve levels of investment that might accelerate economic growth. Low incomes also meant consumer demand inadequate to attract capital investment from other countries. Low levels of investment, in turn, completed the circle of low productivity, low incomes, and backwardness. Low incomes also meant poor housing, poor sanitation, and poor health conditions, which reduced both vigor and length of life and built a young population structure with a large proportion of unproductive dependents. Low incomes, furthermore, precluded innovation in economic affairs. Since innovation requires a surplus on which to rely in case of failure, a peasant family living at subsistence level cannot afford to experiment with new methods or machines; it must be conservative, for one crop failure means death from starvation. Also generating conservatism was the dominance in some underdeveloped areas of an economic elite with large land holdings and high incomes whose savings were usually not invested for national economic development but were used instead for acquiring more land, for money-lending at high rates of interest to the peasants, or for investing in more advanced countries.

Some economists have pointed to economic dualism as another problem in some areas. The Dutch economist J. H. Boecke, for example, in describing the economy of Indonesia under the Dutch, pointed out that a market economy developed in some sectors of the economy under the aegis of European and American capital, that it was tied very closely to the import-export trade, and that it involved only a small part of the population. The bulk of the people remained isolated in a subsistence economy organized around village and family relationships. The two parts of the economy seldom came into contact, and the westernized sector imparted no growth impulse to the native sector.

Economic stagnation is one thing. A declining living standard is quite another — and worse. The grim conditions of underdeveloped areas have been magnified by rapid population growth, which absorbs gains everywhere and sometimes threatens disaster. Birth rates in underdeveloped nations have always been high, but they have been counterbalanced by high death rates until the application of modern methods of sanitation and public health made populations soar. This development made action imperative. The nations themselves have begun to plan for economic growth, devising various methods to increase savings and to mobilize them for economic expansion under the auspices of government. In addition, the Western nations and the Soviet bloc began programs of loans and grants to stimulate economic growth in underdeveloped areas, partly for their own economic benefit, partly for political reasons, and partly on ethical grounds.

Many economists are hopeful that the problem can be solved, that the poor nations can break out of their vicious circle of poverty and set in motion a self-sustaining process of economic growth. For example, the American economist W. W. Rostow argues that any nation goes through a series of stages of economic development as it moves from a traditional society to a modern mass-consumption economy. The process involves establishing certain preconditions — a stable government, improved education, a group of innovators and businessmen to mobilize and use savings, and expanded trade. Then comes the "take-off" into sustained growth, when the economy breaks its shackles and economic progress dominates. Crucial to this change, says Rostow, is an increase in savings and investment to 10 per cent or more of the national income. Finally the development of industry and rising living standards lead to economic maturity and mass consumption.

Implicit in Rostow's analysis is a series of policy recommendations that found great favor in the United States. First, social reform is needed to make the underdeveloped nations more like North America — "Do it the way we did," Rostow says in effect. Second, the concept of the take-off implies that economic aid to developing countries can be gradually phased out, even if it must be initially large to get the take-off started; this aspect of Rostow's ideas has an obvious appeal to the economy-minded. Third, Rostow's description of the growth process implies that once begun, it is not dependent on planning or state management: it is self-sustaining. Perhaps for this reason he titled his book *The Stages of Economic Growth: A Non-Communist Manifesto* (1960). But not even Rostow argued that the process is self-*starting*. It requires cooperative planning by the underdeveloped countries and by the advanced countries who supply capital, with an emphasis on establishing the preconditions and raising the rate of capital accumulation.

Other economists are less optimistic about the prospects for achieving a natural or self-sustaining process of growth. Gunnar Myrdal, the Swedish economist who helped develop the Swedish version of national income theory concurrently with Keynes and who wrote a sociological classic on the American racial problem, *An American Dilemma,* has argued persuasively that the economic gap between advanced and underdeveloped nations is widening. The already industrialized nations have high incomes which generate large amounts of savings, he points out in *An International Economy* (1956), but the savings are not invested in underdeveloped nations because of higher profit rates at home. The industrial economy has reached into some parts of the world with mines and plantations to produce for export, but these economic enclaves draw savings and the most talented people from the local economy, leaving it more starved for the means of achieving growth than it was in the first place. This means, says Myrdal, that underdeveloped nations cannot model themselves on advanced nations but must act radically within their own economies to reorganize imports and exports, diversify production, and plan for economic development.

Myrdal's line of argument was taken one step further by Raúl Prebisch, an Argentine economist who has been working with the United Nations — an example of talent being drawn out of a less developed country. Prebisch argued, and Myrdal supported the point, that the "terms of trade" have a long-run tendency to be unfavorable to underdeveloped areas. These regions produce primary commodities for export—foodstuffs, minerals, and other land-based products—for which markets are highly competitive and which can easily be produced in excess. The result is low prices and low incomes for the producers, as well as highly unstable markets. Advanced countries, on the other hand, export manufactured goods, whose prices tend to rise, according to Prebisch, because of strong monopolistic controls by producers and demands by organized labor for higher wages. These nations, therefore, sell at high prices to underdeveloped areas and buy at low prices from them. This would not be too bad if rising incomes in the advanced countries resulted in a larger demand for the products of the poor countries, but this is not the case: Prebisch has shown that incomes in industrial areas rise almost twice as fast as do their imports.

Prebisch has proposed several solutions. He advocates regional economic integration—common markets, customs unions, free-trade areas, etc.—among groups of underdeveloped countries to widen local markets while retaining tariff protection against imports from advanced nations. Within regional free-trade areas, the nations could plan for industrial growth, having the twin effects of reducing their dependence on foreign manufactures and using more of their primary production domestically. In addition, Prebisch strongly supports international efforts to stabilize the prices of primary products on world markets, and this implies some kind of production restraint or planning in most cases.

The world is faced by a widening gap between rich and poor nations. The economic development process that began in England, moved to the Continent, leaped the Atlantic to North America, and was transplanted to areas like Australia and Japan has not continued its spread to other parts of the world. Indeed, the existence of advanced industrial areas has tended to inhibit the growth of industry elsewhere, at least at the present stage of world economic development. The failure of industrialization to spread evenly across the globe has led poorer nations to see that they must consciously change their environment if they wish even to keep up and possibly to catch up. The example of the Soviet Union shows them what economic planning and heavy sacrifices can accomplish in a relatively short time, although they hope to avoid the authoritarianism of the Stalin regime. Most underdeveloped countries are faced with a clear choice between planning radical changes in their way of life or falling even further behind.

Will Capitalism Survive?

Nikita Khrushchev, the former Soviet premier, once toasted a group of Americans at a Moscow party with the now-famous remark, "We shall bury you." Although the statement was made half jokingly, it has come to symbolize the ideological conflict of our time. Two economic systems are contesting for the loyalties of men, and the rivalry exists at all levels—philosophical, economic, diplomatic, and military. It is expressed in the terms used by both sides: "iron curtain," "cold war," "peoples' democracies," "neoimperialism," and the like. The contest is by no means ended, and economists, seeking as always to fathom the future, have tried to examine the present as a clue to what lies ahead.

JOSEPH SCHUMPETER, PESSIMIST

Joseph Schumpeter (1883–1950) did not think that capitalism would survive. Born in the same year as John Maynard Keynes, Schumpeter was usually bracketed with Keynes as one of the two greatest living economists. Since his death, economic theory has developed in directions other than those taken by Schumpeter, but economists will continue to consider his three major works as valuable historical and theoretical sources. All three books sing the praises of the capitalist entrepreneur, described as the innovating profit-seeker responsible for the constant change that makes a private-enterprise system dynamic.

In his first important book, *The Theory of Economic Development* (1912), Schumpeter presented an analysis of the function of the entrepreneur in creating economic progress and change. The private-enterprise economy always offers large rewards for new products, new production methods, or new systems of organization. The first man to offer lower costs or new products with customer appeal earns high profits. The entrepreneur is that first man, and his continual innovation is the source of the growth and change that is characteristic of modern capitalist society.

Schumpeter carried the analysis a step further in *Business Cycles* (1939), where he argued that innovations tend to be bunched at certain times—one leading to another—creating large investment booms that promote long periods of prosperity. When investment declines from these high levels, the prosperous years are succeeded by stagnation and bad times. Superimposed on these "long waves" of economic activity are business cycles as we know them: during a long wave of good times prosperity is sustained and strong and the down-turns short and shallow, while just the opposite effects occur during the long periods of bad times. In the process, the series of industrial revolutions characteristic of capitalism occur, each one ushering in a long period of good times rooted in a group of related innovations.

The book was one answer to the pessimists who felt that the Great Depression of the 1930's marked the ultimate failure of capitalism. Schumpeter's argument implied that the system was only in one of the troughs of its long waves and that a better future was in store as innovation and technological change turned the wave upward once more. The book also expressed Shumpeter's view of the inner dynamics of capitalism and his answer to Marx. The bad effects of capitalism were not the result of its faults but were caused by its strengths. The innovating, profit-seeking activity of the entrepreneur brought change, growth, and expansion, but the process was erratic rather than smooth and steady, and one result was the business cycle.

This theme—that the dynamic factors in capitalism lead to its inadequacies—Schumpeter developed in his finest book, *Capitalism, Socialism, and Democracy* (1942). He believed strongly in the effectiveness of capitalism in producing goods and services for all and estimated that the fifty years from 1928 to 1978 would see a more than doubled output in the United States, making it possible to eliminate poverty for all but the exceptional "pathological" case. In the process, however, several social characteristics of capitalism would become apparent.

One characteristic is the gradual elimination of the entrepreneur.

The technology and organization of large-scale production are important innovations of capitalism, leading to big business and monopolistic markets. The bureaucracies created to run large enterprises are not places where individualistic, innovating entrepreneurs can function. These men are lone operators, dreamers of large schemes, and risk-takers, while bureaucracies tend to be run by committees, by people who conserve the status quo rather than change it. The very organizations created by entrepreneurs dispense with their services.

A second characteristic of developing capitalism predicted by Schumpeter is the alienation of intellectuals from adherence to the system. Thinkers, writers, and teachers are critics of the existing order, even though their position is made possible by the affluence of capitalist society. Their function is to point out faults in an effort to make the world better, and they succeed in creating a climate of opinion antagonistic to the capitalist way of life.

This environment of public opinion engenders a third characteristic, government intervention in economic affairs. The intervention is directed toward the faults of the economy—toward reducing inequality, smoothing out the business cycle, reducing speculation, controlling monopoly, subsidizing agriculture, and so forth. As a by-product, it also reduces the entrepreneur's freedom of action and serves to further reduce the dynamism of the economy.

These trends in economic organization, the climate of opinion, and public policy lead to the gradual elimination of the entrepreneur from economic life, and with him the economic advances that give capitalism its appeal. The growth of the economy is hindered, capitalism loses its ability to satisfy new wants, and the predictions of collapse made by the intellectuals are fulfilled. As the performance of the system becomes poorer, government intervention increases, which further reduces the vitality of the system and makes socialism inevitable. Schumpeter believed that socialism would replace capitalism in the long run and that it could be either democratic or authoritarian in political structure—the great choice of the future lay in the political sphere. To the question "Can capitalism survive?" Schumpeter answered, "No. I do not think it can."

ECONOMIC GROWTH AFTER WORLD WAR II

Schumpeter's pessimistic predictions about the future of capitalism have not materialized. The advanced industrial nations that still base their economies primarily on private ownership of the means of production—the United States, Canada, Great Britain, France, West Germany, Italy, and Japan—have experienced since World War II a period of prosperity and growth unmatched in their previous history.

Those nations as a group, with an aggregate population of about 500 million, more than doubled their total output of products and services between 1949 and 1963. Investment in plant and equipment more than doubled. The number of automobiles and telephones in use more than doubled, the average length of the work week was reduced, agricultural production rose by a little less than 50 per cent, living standards increased in all seven countries, and notable advances were made in education, health, and scientific research. The national advances did not proceed at the same pace in each country—the Japanese economy has grown most rapidly and that of Great Britain the slowest. Western Europe in general has grown more rapidly than the United States. But the differences among the seven advanced countries are much less than their contrast with underdeveloped areas, which have tended to fall further behind.

One of the most important reasons for this advance has been the investment boom set in motion by the scientific developments of World War II, particularly in such industries as electronics, plastics, and atomic energy, and by the coming of age of the automobile as the most important form of transportation. Schumpeter would have been quite at home with this development, pointing out that one discovery leads to another, one innovation fosters others, one adaptation stimulates a second, and so on. The result is a whole new world of automobiles, jet aircraft, computers, automated production, and extended urbanization, which has created vast areas of economic opportunity.

Schumpeter did not foresee a second factor, however—the research revolution. Innovation has become an integral part of business enterprise and public activity. Basic and applied research has expanded manyfold over the level of the 1920's and 1930's and has become an accepted function of both business and government. This research and development—the basic ingredient of innovation—provides a new dynamism to the whole economic system, even though much of it has been associated with military needs and the race for the moon.

A third factor in the postwar expansion has been the emergence of the consumer to a position of even greater importance. As incomes rose, more consumers had larger amounts of "discretionary" income over and above the amounts needed for satisfying basic wants, which enabled them to invest in homes and home furnishings, automobiles, and other durable goods and in securities and insurance policies. Recreational industries expanded as people gained larger amounts of leisure time, and service industries grew. The "powerful consumer" was a greater determinant of the level and mix of economic activity than ever before.

These developments on the economic scene would not have stimulated the postwar boom unless business firms were willing and able to take advantage of them. They proved eager to do so. Although many economists feared a postwar slump, the lifting of wartime controls in country after country in 1945–1946 provided scope for business action that had not been present for more than fifteen years, not since the depression had first shackled the businessman. The business and financial community seized the opportunities created by elimination of wage and price controls and wartime allocations of supplies and labor, by high consumer incomes, and by a huge backlog of unmet consumer demand. Investments, plant capacity, and prices rose; economic expansion was rapid. Indeed, the boom was strong enough to create inflationary pressures that lasted for a dozen years.

This freeing of business enterprise also occurred in the international economy. Many of the trade restrictions that had been imposed during the interwar period were removed by establishing the General Agreement on Tariffs and Trade and the European Common Market, and wider freedom for international trade and movement of capital, and therefore prosperity for the capitalist nations, were established.

The policy of freeing business enterprise from restrictions was supplemented by government efforts to promote high levels of economic activity. Acceptance of the Keynesian point of view by policymakers in all of the advanced countries meant that government took responsibility for the maintenance of high levels of employment and acceptable rates of economic growth. The new attitude was typified by passage of the Employment Act of 1946 in the United States:

> The Congress declares that it is the continuing policy and responsibility of the Federal Government to use all practicable means . . . for the purpose of creating and maintaining . . . conditions under which there will be afforded useful employment opportunities . . . for those able, willing and seeking to work, and to promote maximum employment, production and purchasing power.

A variety of techniques has been developed to implement these policies. Government spending, which reached high levels during World War II, was cut back severely after the war when consumer demand and business investment reached high levels. A policy of easy money was adopted to stimulate growth in the private sector of the economy, at least to the extent that inflationary pressures would allow. When recessions threaten, it is now part of the accepted pattern either to increase government expenditures to fill the gap left by the decline in the private sector or to reduce taxes to give an added stimulus to private spending and investment. The goal has been to balance the economy at full employment levels rather than to balance government budgets, and the budget is used as a means of achieving that economic balance. The ideal situation is seen as one in which the economy operates at full employment, with stable prices and a balanced government budget that neither stimulates the economy to inflationary levels nor holds it back at less than full employment.

These policy goals are often difficult to achieve. The existence of large monopoloid business firms and equally powerful labor unions has made the preservation of stable prices quite difficult in several countries, particularly since those two parties know that, whatever bargain they make among themselves, their government is committed to full employment. Inflation is always a danger when an economy is operating at or near capacity, and the various causes of price increases are only imperfectly understood and not easily controlled. Nevertheless, all the major industrial nations have been moving toward more effective anti-inflation measures to supplement their commitment to full employment.

Technological change also creates problems, particularly for displaced workers and for those with relatively little skill or education. Most capitalist countries have embarked on major manpower training and labor market adjustment programs to meet that problem.

Since not all regions necessarily share in the economic advances of even the most rapidly growing economies, development programs have been instituted in backward regions of countries like Italy and France, many of them modeled after the highly successful Tennessee Valley Authority in the United States.

Thus, prosperity has its problems, too, and they have not been ignored in the formulation of economic policy. Despite the problems, however, the post-World War II economic surge has brought Western civilization to heights of prosperity that bring nearer to realization the age-old dream of ending poverty. It was an economist, John Kenneth Galbraith, who may have named this new world when he named his book *The Affluent Society* (1958).

The post-World War II expansion, together with the Soviet challenge and the problems of underdeveloped nations, made economic growth once more a central subject of economics. Economists sought again, as they had in the eighteenth and early nineteenth centuries, to understand the sources of growth and the means by which a sustained process of growth could be achieved. The mercantilists, physiocrats, and liberals had wrestled with the same problem, but the contemporary discussion has been far more scientific and much less concerned with ideological issues and the special interests of powerful political groups.

The most important theoretical analysis was worked out independently by R. F. Harrod and Evsey Domar at Oxford and Johns Hopkins universities. Like the classical economists, they stressed the crucial role of capital investment in increasing production capacity, but they also pointed to its function of generating income. These two effects of investment must balance each other if the economy is to grow evenly. Thus if productive capacity grows more rapidly than incomes, unemployment and unused resources will appear, and the rate of investment will not be sustained. Conversely, if incomes grow faster than output capacity, inflation will eventually result from the excess purchasing power and will in time hamper investment.

The problem of balance is compounded by the fact that growth requires continually larger amounts of investment. This year's savings, channeled into investment, result in enlarged incomes next year; larger incomes produce greater savings, which must in turn be offset by enlarged investment; and enlarged investment creates greater output capacity, the products of which must be sold if investment is to continue to grow. Maintaining an equilibrium between growth of income and expansion of output capacity is no easy task. Both Harrod and Domar stated that the equilibrium does not occur automatically, and both implied that monetary and fiscal measures are needed to sustain full employment growth. Like the Keynesian economics from which it was derived, this post-Keynesian theory of economic growth supported the policies that were in fact being developed during the postwar years.

THE CHANGING ECONOMIC SYSTEM

The tremendous post-World War II growth of the industrial nations brought with it large changes in the economic system. Rooted in earlier developments, these recent changes have been so far-reaching that it has become fashionable to call even the American economy "mixed" rather than capitalistic.

The old image of capitalism stressed the competition among profit-seeking enterprises that produced the goods and services demanded by consumers. Private business firms were considered to be the source of innovations and investments responsible for change and growth. The unremitting pressure of self-interest was held to be the driving force behind the whole system, resting on the solid base of private ownership and control of the means of production. Government had only a minor role, primarily that of establishing the rules of the game and assuring the preservation of competition. Above all, the private sector was presented as the dynamic, moving force of the economy.

Much of this picture remains valid for an economy like that of the United States, but much also has changed. The rise of big business and big labor has given private economic units a good deal of control over both markets and resources. Big government uses and produces on a large scale, and its influence in some sectors of the economy is very great. Even if capitalism can be said to survive, its face has changed.

One of the most important studies of the changing nature of the modern economy was *The Modern Corporation and Private Property* (1932) by Adolf A. Berle, Jr., and Gardner C. Means. It documented the dominant position of the large corporation in the modern economy, the growing dispersion of ownership of corporate stock, and the separation of ownership from control. Emphasis was placed on the new structure of power that had appeared, in which the officers of corporations dominated policies while owning only insignificant portions of the stock. The book also questioned the continued validity of the traditional "logic of profits": since profits went to owners rather than to decision-makers, production decisions were no longer necessarily in accord with consumer wishes. The close connections between consumer wants, profits, and business decisions were seriously loosened. Instead, business decisions might reflect the needs of management and the ability of their firms to control markets.

The two authors continued to develop these themes in later studies. Berle has developed two chief ideas in a series of articles and books, the most important of which were *The 20th Century Capitalist Revolution* (1954), *Power Without Property* (1959), and *The American Economic Republic* (1963). The first idea is that the new place of the corporation in the economy has given big business both a public function and public responsibilities, which in turn has caused the firm and its management to exercise its economic power with restraint, to accept its public functions, and to modify its quest for profit. The second idea is that the nature of private property has changed significantly. Property in the hands of powerful corporations, because of its essentially public nature, is no longer private in the old sense, and the power it brings to those who control it can no longer be exercised freely, with regard only to private interests. As a result, we are moving toward a new relationship in which public interests prevail over private. As Berle sees it:

> American society is not being used by, but, rather, uses the profit-seeking market-enterprise system, and certainly is not governed by it. Private enterprise in the United States is thus essentially an instrument of the state — not, as was formerly believed (perhaps accurately), an end for which the state exists.

In other words, property has remained private while its use has been partly socialized.

Gardner Means has pursued other aspects of the place of big business in the economy, concentrating on prices and pricing policy. In 1934 he originated the term "administered prices" to describe the type of prices found in monopoloid sectors of the economy.[1] Means showed that such prices were relatively inflexible and did not respond readily to changes in demand. When demand fell during the depression years, certain firms maintained their prices and cut output and employment. This relative freedom from the effects of market forces, together with the prevalence of large corporations, has created a new type of economic system. According to Means in a later work, *The Corporate Revolution in America* (1964):

> We now have single corporate enterprises employing hundreds of thousands of workers, having hundreds of thousands of stockholders, using billions of dollars' worth of the instruments of production, serving millions of customers, and controlled by a single management group. These are great collectives of enterprise, and a system composed of them might well be called "collective capitalism."

Means, as well as Berle, seems to be saying that government ownership is not the only path to socialism but that corporate enterprise is taking us there by other routes.

If there was any doubt about the importance of big enterprise and the monopoloid nature of many sectors of the American economy, it was dispelled by the reports of the Temporary National Economic Committee that were published in the early 1940's. This joint congressional committee investigated the concentration of economic power in the United States in the late 1930's. Its hundreds of volumes of testimony and forty-three expert monographs documented the overwhelming importance of the large corporation, particularly in finance, transportation, heavy industry, and durable consumer goods manufacturing.

Many other studies by economists and government agencies have examined the large corporation and its impact on the economy, but few have raised such fundamental questions as have Berle and Means or documented the place of big business as well as the TNEC studies. They showed that the rise of big business, separation of ownership and control, and the impact of corporate decisions on workers, customers, and the public raise new issues of social power and control. The ends to which that power is to be used and the goals which the economic system is to pursue become decisions that can be very largely influenced, if not controlled completely, by conscious actions. Economics has become political economy once more. The very organization of productive enterprise has made laissez faire obsolete. Even if government did not seek to control economic activity, big business would.

If Berle and Means and the TNEC were worried about the power

[1] The term was used in a confidential memorandum to the Secretary of Agriculture that was "leaked" to the press and to Congress and later published as "Industrial Prices and Their Relative Flexibility," U.S. Senate Document 13, 74th Congress, 1st Session.

of big business and its management, Sumner H. Slichter was concerned with labor unions. This astute observer of the American economy argued that "a laboristic society is succeeding a capitalistic one." Power was shifting from business to labor as employees organized themselves into labor unions — "the most powerful economic organizations of the time" — to bargain collectively with management. Slichter pointed out in *Union Policies and Industrial Management* (1941) that bargaining between unions and management had developed a system of industrial jurisprudence that had largely replaced free market relationships in determining the rights of the two parties and their economic gains. In *Trade Unions in a Free Society* (1947) he took up the problem of the relationship of unions to the operation of free institutions. This well-reasoned book came at a time when the general public and Congress were also vitally interested in the problem — the Taft-Hartley Act was passed in the same year — but the political debate was polarized around extremes of opinion about unions and lacked the even-tempered appraisal that Slichter brought to the issue. He was neither for nor against labor organizations but recognized that responsible unions and cooperative union-management relations could be a great force for social good, while selfish and narrow viewpoints on either side could severely damage the economy and the social order as a whole. The problems were to keep conflict at a minimum, to assure a fair distribution of freedom and opportunity, to limit abuses of power, and to achieve a satisfactory balance between individual and community interests. Slichter offered no solutions, but it was clear from his analysis that these problems would not solve themselves. Again, an economist was suggesting that wise social policies were required to correlate the emerging economic institutions of mid-century with the broad goals of society.

The growth of big business and big labor has been paralleled by the growth of big government. This has been one of the most heavily publicized changes in the American economy, with much of the publicity coming from the business community as part of its opposition to the trend. The opposition has sometimes maintained that the growth of government economic activity has been an alien development foisted on an unwilling society by political adventurers and demagogues, but economists have produced different explanations.

Solomon Fabricant, for example, in his scholarly study *The Trend of Government Activity in the United States Since 1900* (1952), argued that economic growth itself was the chief reason for the expanded role of government. Population growth and its changing structure, the end of the frontier, advancing science and technology, urbanization and industrialization, the growing size of business enterprise, and growing economic interdependence — these developments created new problems that the free market could not easily solve and that demanded new government functions at all levels, federal, state, and local. Added stimuli were provided by recurring depressions, wars, and the increased possibilty of war. Finally, Fabricant pointed out that the climate of opinion has changed: there is growing confidence in the ability of governments to meet new needs, confidence inspired in part by improved organization and efficiency within government itself. He noted that by mid-century the government was the nation's biggest banker, operated the largest insurance company, employed one eighth of the labor force, exerted a major influence on wage and salary levels, and was the largest single buyer of commodities. He expected this share in economic activity to become larger as the economy expanded and incomes grew.

It has. Fifteen years later Eli Ginsberg and his research associates, in *The Pluralistic Economy* (1965), showed that private profit-seeking enterprises — the traditional subjects of much economic theory and the central institution of capitalism — now share the scene with two other types of economic organization. One is the limited-profit enterprise like public utilities and other regulated firms, defense industries, and government-subsidized private enterprise. The other is the "not-for-profit" sector, which includes hospitals, universities, religious enterprises (such as publishers of religious books), and governments at all levels. Focusing on the latter group, Ginsberg showed that the not-for-profit sector accounts for about one fourth of the nation's income and up to two fifths of its employment. It is a major contributor to innovation and technical change, and it employs two thirds of the nation's professional and technical manpower. In recent years it was the most rapidly growing sector of the economy: between 1950 and 1960 nine out of every ten new jobs reflected, directly or indirectly, the expansion of the not-for-profit sector.

The growth of large public and private organizations in the economy has made it clear that the impersonal operation of market forces is now supplemented by the ability of important groups in labor, management, and government to influence significantly the way the economy functions. Political and economic power, its organization and its locus, influence economic decisions as never before. Yet the new order has not developed an explanation of how it operates, although a suggestion was given by John Kenneth Galbraith in his book *American Capitalism* (1952). Galbraith argued that the economic system of large organizations works effectively only because of the existence of "countervailing power" — that is, one center of economic power is unable to exploit the rest of the economy because other centers of power arise to limit its influence. Big business begets big labor, and large manufacturers beget large retailers and large suppliers of raw materials, according to Galbraith. Government stands as a balance wheel, ready to step in if any one economic power center becomes too important. In this way an orderly pattern of decision-making emerges out of potential chaos and conflict. Bargaining between small numbers of equally powerful organizations replaces the system of self-adjusting markets as the essential element in the economic system. Is this capitalism? Well, perhaps. But it is at best a greatly modified capitalism, quite different from the capitalism of the nineteenth century and earlier, and one that is continuing to change in the direction of larger economic units.

CHANGING TECHNOLOGY

A revolution in technology has accompanied the revolution in organization. Called *automation,* it represents a major new element on the economic scene. Yet today's automation is only the latest of the twentieth-century transformations in industrial production that have been carrying to their logical conclusions such earlier developments as assembly-line mass production, scientific management, and the rationalization of industry. Machines have been substituted for men for generations, and part of the progress made by mankind over the centuries has taken the form of mechanical slaves to do the work formerly done by people.

But where earlier forms of mechanization generally organized work better (the assembly line), or substituted mechanical power for human or animal energy (the steam engine and electricity), or combined the two (the steel-rolling mill), the new technology uses electrical impulses to replace human senses and the human mind. In this respect today's technology is truly revolutionary. At present it is theoretically possible to automate any process that transforms inputs into outputs and to control that process with computers. Whether or not a specific process is so treated depends on the economics of the situation, but the theoretical principles and much of the technology are available.

Process control by computers—what has come to be called *cybernation*—is at the heart of the technological transformation. Automatic operation of production processes only began the transformation. Combinations of automatic operation and computer control have been able to eliminate human effort almost entirely in some kinds of production processes, and at this early stage we can only speculate about the ultimate result.

The origins of automation are to be found just prior to the Second World War in the automobile industry, where engineers began experimenting with automatic production lines. In the case of an engine block, for example, the machining job was performed by man-operated machine tools, then the partly finished block was moved to the next station where another operation was carried out, and so on. Machines to move the engine block from station to station were easy enough to develop, but engineers were unable to automatically position the block in relation to the machine tool precisely enough that the machining operation could be carried out automatically within the narrow tolerances required for internal-combustion engines. There was no adequate substitute for human senses aided by mechanical measuring devices.

The substitute was developed in principle by the Navy just before World War II and adopted during the war in radar-controlled anti-aircraft guns. The Navy's problem was that attacking airplanes came at ships too fast for humans to shoot down. Engineers successfully developed electronic devices to sense enemy planes, feed the information to control mechanisms, and fire guns automatically. The principle of feedback of "sensory" preceptions to an automatic control mechanism had been successfully applied.

After the war, engineers in the automobile industry applied this feedback principle to their production problems. Huge transfer machines, 500–700 feet long, carried out automatically more than a hundred individual processing jobs. These machines are actually a whole series of machines, linked together by transfer mechanisms, each one automatically controlled by a series of measuring devices and *servomechanisms* that sense the item to be processed, position it properly, direct the operation of the tool unit, and test the product after each step. The transfer mechanisms then move the item on to the next station for another operation. The control devices are variously mechanical, hydraulic, or electrical in operation, but each similarly replaces human perceptions.

Although the development of highly sophisticated feedback systems was a tremendous advance over the usual assembly-line operation, their application was limited primarily to mass production lines that turned out large numbers of identical or nearly identical products. The major revolution in technology took place when electronic computers were constructed to control production and information systems—to replace human intelligence just as automatic control mechanisms had replaced man's senses and transfer mechanisms his muscle.

The age of computer control has arrived. Many kinds of production systems have been equipped with automatic machinery controlled by computers programmed to operate the system in a variety of ways. In cement production, for example, limestone, clay, and other raw materials are brought together in a kiln where they are roasted; the output is cement in powdered form, which is then bagged or otherwise prepared for shipment. The general pattern for production of most commodities and services is:

Inputs ⟶ Process ⟶ Outputs

When computers are used to control the process, however, the pattern changes:

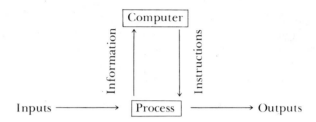

Information from the process is fed into the computer, which assimilates it in its program and relays it back to the process as instructions. The transfer of information and instructions is effected in much less time than it takes to read this brief description. The computer can also report to management on the results of the operation at the very moment that the outputs are emerging.

Cybernated processes like this have been developed in many sectors of the economy. Cybernated grocery stores are now in operation in several European countries. The first cybernated warehouses are now functioning. Completely automatic, computer-controlled production processes have been developed in a variety of industries: oil production, petroleum refining, chemicals manufacturing, cement production, steel manufacturing, and even in several assembly operations. Much of the work in business offices and banks is now computer controlled. Computers can also be taught to solve problems and make decisions, such as designing an entire chemical plant, selecting the location of a manufacturing plant, or determining the prices at which overstocked merchandise should be sold.

The use of computers has only begun but certainly will spread as new applications are devised and as more powerful and less costly units are developed. Computer control has already been applied in all aspects of economic life, as the preceding illustrations indicate, and, at present, limitations on their use are economic rather than technical. Computers have made it theoretically possible to virtually eliminate human effort from the production process. In the not too distant future, man may be a superior being who directs a mass of production machines, controls, and computers, much as science fiction books describe. Robots have come of age.

The impact of the new technology on economics has been varied. It has opened up great new mathematical techniques for research and has widened the theoretical boundaries of economics and of all the social sciences. Computers have made possible the solution of quantitative problems that would otherwise have taken hundreds of persons many years to solve. This has enabled economists to construct many-dimensioned models of the economy, based on actual data, and to determine the interrelationships of the components with a high degree of accuracy. *Econometrics* has replaced the older forms of statistics as the basis of much economic research and analysis. Familiarity with mathematical notation and reasoning has also led to their use in theoretical studies. Mathematical models have been used to define problems precisely, to analyze theoretical relationships, to define areas in which additional factual information is needed, and to state carefully the assumptions upon which conclusions are based. One of the landmark books in economics of the postwar years restated the existing body of economic theory in mathematical form—Paul Samuelson's *Foundations of Economic Analysis* (1947)—and in recent years mathematical analysis has been particularly useful in defining sustainable paths of economic growth and the production relationships between and within industries.

The new technology has also fostered new ways of thinking about the nature of economic processes and the economic order. The economy can be viewed as a comprehensive system, with inputs processed into outputs and controlled by a complex decision-making mechanism; economics then becomes a branch of *systems theory*. Alternatively, emphasis may be placed on the various organized units that comprise the economy—families, corporations, unions, governments—which may be analyzed like any other organization, and this part of economics can be considered a branch of *organization theory*. Similarly, other aspects of economics become part of *information theory, decision theory, conflict theory*, and so on, as the various aspects of systems and organizations are broken down for detailed study. Similar developments have taken place in all the social sciences: new theoretical sciences overlap the older disciplines, while the traditional sciences become applied fields of study. A high level of scientific generalization has been made possible by the new technology.

The most important effect of the new technology on economics has been in the realm of public policy. An economy of automation and computer control, together with a predominance of large organizations, raises the most fundamental of questions in a democratic society. If machines can perform various tasks more quickly and accurately than people, the value of the individual is called into question; important psychological problems could arise if men and women come to feel that they are of little worth. In a technologically based economy there is a danger that decisions will be made on the basis of what is best for technology, not what is best for people. Moreover, a highly complex technology requires a core of specially trained managers and technicians whose expertise is not widely known and whose strategic positions could enable them to gain political power and use it in an authoritarian fashion, as visualized by Aldous Huxley in *Brave New World* and by George Orwell in *1984*.

Whether or not these gloomy possibilities become actual, it is certain that the increased productive powers of the economy will bring about changed attitudes toward work and leisure. Vastly increased productivity will make possible much higher standards of living and greatly reduced hours of work. The necessity to work may be altogether eliminated for many people, and others may find that technological advances have usurped all the positions for which they once qualified. Should that occur—and such economists as Kenneth Galbraith and Robert Theobald have pointed to the possibility—new patterns of income distribution may have to be developed. Galbraith has suggested permanent unemployment insurance, and Theobald has proposed guaranteed incomes as the only way to preserve the economic system under such conditions.

The surest promise of the new technology is economic abundance—abundance of both necessities and luxuries. In advanced industrial nations, at least, poverty as we know it can be virtually ended. There is reassuring evidence, furthermore, that economic gains from modern technology can and will be used wisely. The increased incomes and leisure time available to Americans during the past half-century have brought vast improvements in the quality of life: literature, music, art, and the theater are thriving as never before; more people are better educated; and the mass media are potentially capable of bringing to millions education and entertainment that were available only to a select minority a few generations ago. The promise is often greater than the accomplishment, but the promise carries hope.

THE CHALLENGES AHEAD

The world of the twentieth century is a world of large organizations and giant economic units, a world in which governments are increasingly important in the affairs of men, a world of computers and robots, a world of challenges, the responses to which will determine the way men live for the next era in human history.

One challenge is that of world peace. Modern weapons will have to be brought under effective control. The ideological conflicts that now divide the world could erupt into nuclear conflicts that destroy the material advances of thousands of years, if not all life itself. Past conflicts of great magnitude have been reconciled, however. Sixteenth-century Europe, for example, was torn by strife between two seemingly irreconcilable religious ideologies. Protestant and Catholic murdered each other with fanatic vigor, and the Continent was divided into two armed camps for a hundred years. Yet from beneath the surface a new world emerged—a capitalistic market economy, a system of national states, and a social structure dominated by a middle class. At the end of that hundred years the basis for continued ideological struggle was gone. The modern world faces a somewhat similar situation. While men argue heatedly over capitalism and communism, over democracy and authority, a changing world again makes the debate increasingly irrelevant. One great hope is that the developments of the new era—big organization, a computerized technology, and a social structure dominated by white-collar bureaucracies—will in the future make the contending systems more like each other and thereby weaken the sources of international conflict. But whether or not this convergence occurs, it is imperative that better methods be developed for resolving the conflicts inherent in large political units equipped with the most advanced means of destruction.

A second challenge is posed by large-scale organization and modern technology. If democratic values are to prevail, means must be found to preserve people's rights and individuality. This is no mean task, for it will require structuring the organization of business, labor, government, and education to provide a maximum of freedom while retaining the ability of large organizations to operate effectively. It may be that individualism and bureaucracy are ultimately incompatible, but an effort to reconcile the two has not been made on anything like the scale required.

Finally, there is the challenge of abundance. It is now possible to produce at a level that can bring wealth to even the poorest men and women, but whether and how well this is done will determine the quality of life for all. At the moment we appear not to be doing too well: violence rises while smog settles and water supplies fall, urban congestion increases, billboards and junk yards multiply along the highways, the impersonality of life in large organizations is discussed even in comic strips, nervousness grows, and hostility deepens. Something is seriously wrong with the way abundance is being used. In some countries abundance is yet to be achieved, and unchecked population growth may prevent its achievement for many generations.

Perhaps these issues are only what might have been expected. The problems one generation has been able to solve lead to the difficulties another must face. The contemporary economist feels that he knows what must be done to operate the economy at high levels and to foster a satisfactory rate of economic growth, but he is less sure about how the fruits can be divided equitably and about what ought to be done with the enormous output. Like Alice's croquet mallets that kept turning into flamingos, answers in economics keep turning into more questions. The age of the economist continues, along with the quest for the good life.

138

SUGGESTIONS FOR FURTHER READING

The literature of economics is vast and complex. It is no longer possible for even professional economists to be familiar with all of it, although a century ago a man like Karl Marx could devote a lifetime to the subject and read just about everything that had been written in the field.

There are some good textbook surveys of the history of economics. The more readable of these comprehensive works are Erich Roll, *A History of Economic Thought*, 3rd ed. (Englewood Cliffs, N.J.: Prentice-Hall, Inc., 1956); John F. Bell, *A History of Economic Thought* (New York: Ronald Press, 1953); and Charles Gide and Charles Rist, *A History of Economic Doctrines*, 2nd ed. (Boston: D. C. Heath and Co., 1948). Two surveys interesting for their points of view are Leo Rogin, *The Meaning and Validity of Economic Theory* (New York: Harper and Brothers, 1956), which emphasizes the uses to which economic theories are put, and Joseph Schumpeter, *A History of Economic Analysis* (New York: Oxford University Press, 1954), an encyclopedic volume that stresses the development of economics as a science.

The early history of capitalism is covered in the standard treatises on the economic history of Europe, but few analyze the rise of the market economy. Two books that do are Karl Polanyi, *The Great Transformation* (Boston: Beacon Press, 1957) and Richard H. Tawney's great work, *Religion and the Rise of Capitalism* (New York: New American Library, 1947).

The Industrial Revolution has been interpreted in a variety of ways. Two classics are Paul Mantoux, *The Industrial Revolution in the Eighteenth Century* (New York: Torch Books, Harper and Row, 1962) and Arnold Toynbee, *Lectures on the Industrial Revolution in England* (Boston: Beacon Press, 1956). Two more recent brief treatments are Thomas S. Ashton, *The Industrial Revolution, 1760–1830* (London: Oxford University Press, 1948) and Dorothy George, *England in Transition* (London: Pelican Books, 1953). A well-selected group of readings from the classical economists and their critics is John Bowditch and Clement Ramsland, eds., *Voices of the Industrial Revolution* (Ann Arbor: University of Michigan Press, 1961). The relationships between economic ideas and society during the nineteenth century are vividly portrayed in two recent books: E. P. Thompson, *The Making of the English Working Class* (London: Victor Gollancz, 1963) and Cecil Woodham-Smith, *The Great Hunger* (New York: Harper and Row, 1962), which deals with the mid-century Irish famine and efforts to deal with it.

A good compendium that gives the flavor of mercantilism, physiocracy, and early economic liberalism is Arthur E. Monroe, *Early Economic Thought* (Cambridge, Mass.: Harvard University Press, 1945).

A recent paperback edition of Bernard Mandeville's *The Fable of the Bees* (New York: Capricorn Books, 1962) has made this work available to modern readers.

There is a large literature on classical economics. The very best discussion is Wesley Mitchell, *Lecture Notes on Types of Economic Theory* (New York: Augustus M. Kelley, 1966), which originally appeared in mimeographed form during the 1930's; it consists of notes taken from Mitchell's lectures at Columbia University and has the unique characteristic of being equally absorbing for both specialists and the general reader. A more demanding book, but one well worth studying, is Werner Stark, *The Ideal Foundations of Economic Thought* (New York: Oxford University Press, 1944). The best readily available editions of the major works of classical economics are the Modern Library Giant edition of Adam Smith's *Wealth of Nations*; the Ann Arbor Paperbacks edition of Thomas Malthus' *Population: The First Essay*, and the Irwin paperback edition of David Ricardo's *Principles of Political Economy and Taxation*. Smith is not easy to read, Malthus is a delight, and Ricardo is quite difficult. Perhaps the best overall survey of classical economics for the general reader is John Stuart Mill, *Principles of Political Economy*, which is available in most good libraries. Mill's *Autobiography* is a fascinating account of his education and early life, and *The Life of John Stuart Mill* by Michael St. John Packe (New York: The Macmillan Company, 1954) is well worth reading. John Rae, *The Life of Adam Smith* (New York: Augustus M. Kelley, 1965; first published in 1895) is rich in information but not written in a very interesting style. There are no good biographies of either Malthus or Ricardo, but useful brief accounts of their lives are Keynes' essay on Malthus in his *Essays and Sketches in Biography* (New York: Meridian Books, 1956), which also contains interesting accounts of Alfred Marshall and William Stanley Jevons, and "A Memoir of Ricardo," written by one of his brothers and published with addenda in Piero Sraffa, ed., *The Works and Correspondence of David Ricardo*, Vol. X (Cambridge, Eng.: Cambridge University Press, 1955). A fine account of Jeremy Bentham and his influence is Elie Halevy, *The Growth of Philosophic Radicalism* (Boston: Beacon Press, 1955), and classic accounts of Bentham, James Mill, and John Stuart Mill are in Leslie Stephen, *The English Utilitarians* (London: Duckworth and Co., 1900; reprinted by the London School of Economics and Political Science in 1950). Two books that deal effectively with the differences between classical and modern liberalism are Harry K. Girvetz, *The Evolution of Liberalism* (New York: Collier Books, 1963) and William D. Grampp, *Economic Liberalism*, 2 vols. (New York: Random House, 1965).

There are several good introductions to socialist thought. Probably the most interesting and stimulating is Edmund Wilson, *To the Finland Station* (Garden City, N.Y.: Doubleday and Co., Inc., 1953). Two more comprehensive surveys are Harry W. Laidler, *Social-Economic Movements* (New York: Thomas Y. Crowell Co., 1948) and Philip Taft, *Movements for Economic Reform* (New York: Rinehart and Company, Inc., 1950). A fine selection of readings from the socialist literature is in Albert Fried and Ronald Sanders, eds., *Socialist Thought: A Documentary History* (Garden City, N.Y.: Anchor Books, 1964). Peter Kropotkin's *Memoirs of a Revolutionist* (London: Swan, Sonnenschein and Co., 1906) is a very human document, written by one of the leading anarchists, that gives fascinating insights into the socialist movement in its heyday.

The most readily available edition of Marx is the Modern Library Giant edition of the first volume of *Capital*, and a fine translation of all three volumes has recently been published by the Foreign Languages Publishing House in Moscow. The novice should not tackle *Capital* directly, however. A better place to start is *Capital and Other Writings* (New York: Modern Library, 1932), which presents a more logical sequence of the argument. Even that analysis should be read in conjunction with Paul M. Sweezy, *The Theory of Capitalist Development* (New York: Oxford University Press, 1942), which is the best summary of Marxist economics available in English. The best biography of Marx is Franz Mehring, *Karl Marx: The Story of His Life* (London: George Allen and Unwin, 1936). The philosophical background of Marxism is analyzed in Sidney Hook, *From Hegel to Marx* (New York: Humanities Press, 1958), and the Marxist theory of history is admirably treated in M. M. Bober, *Karl Marx's Interpretation of History* (New York: W. W. Norton and Co., 1965). Friedrich Engels' classic work, *The Condition of the Working Class in England in 1844* (London: George Allen and Unwin, 1952; first published in 1845) presents the picture of early industrial capitalism that Marx had in mind when he wrote *Capital*; it is essential reading for anyone who wishes to understand Marxism.

This book did not discuss later Marxist writings, some of which are fascinating and important. Basic Marxist theory was further developed by V. I. Lenin in *Imperialism: The Highest Stage of Capitalism* (New York: International Publishers, 1933), and Lenin's *State and Revolution* (New York: International Publishers, 1932), is the bible of communist political action. "Revisionist" Marxism received its classic statement in Eduard Bernstein, *Evolutionary Socialism* (New York: Schocken Books, 1961) and was refined in Karl Kautsky, *Social Democracy versus Communism* (New York: Rand School Press, 1946). Leon Trotzky's reply and amplification in *The Defense of Terrorism* (London: George Allen and Unwin, 1921) and *The Permanent Revolution* (New York: Pioneer Publishers, 1965) are especially valuable for the light they throw on the policies followed by the Chinese communists in the 1950's and 1960's.

There are a variety of interesting books on the philosophy of individualism and the environment out of which it emerged. My favorite

141

is Sidney Fine, *Laissez Faire and the General-Welfare State* (Ann Arbor: University of Michigan Press, 1964), closely followed by Richard Hofstadter, *Social Darwinism in American Thought* (Boston: Beacon Press, 1955). A more specialized but equally interesting study is Edward C. Kirkland, *Dream and Thought in the Business Community* (Ithaca, N.Y.: Cornell University Press, 1956). Brief collections of the writings of the individualists and their antagonists include E. David Cronon, *Government and the Economy: Some Nineteenth-Century Views* (New York: Holt, Rinehart and Winston, 1960) and *Democracy and the Gospel of Wealth* (Boston: D. C. Heath and Co., 1949). There are some fascinating histories of the era of great wealth: Charles Francis Adams, Jr., and Henry Adams, *Chapters of Erie* (Ithaca, N.Y.: Great Seal Books, Cornell University Press, 1956); Gustavus Myers, *History of the Great American Fortunes* (New York: Modern Library, 1936); and Matthew Josephson, *The Robber Barons* (New York: Harcourt, Brace and Co., 1934). The flavor of individualism can best be obtained from the protagonists themselves, however: Herbert Spencer, *Social Statics* (London: J. Chapman, 1851); William G. Sumner, *Essays* (New Haven: Yale University Press, 1934); and Andrew Carnegie, *Triumphant Democracy* (New York: Charles Scribner's Sons, 1886), *The Gospel of Wealth* (New York: The Century Co., 1900), *The Empire of Business* (New York: Doubleday, Page and Co., 1902), and *Autobiography* (Boston: Houghton Mifflin Company, 1920).

There is no good general survey of neoclassical economics and very little interpretive literature below the scholarly level. Alfred Marshall's *Principles of Economics*, 8th ed. (London: Macmillan and Co., 1920) is ponderous but not difficult; it remains the authoritative statement of the neoclassical system. Three small volumes in the Cambridge Economic Handbook series (Chicago: University of Chicago Press) are a better introduction: Hubert Henderson, *Supply and Demand* (1958); E. A. G. Robinson, *The Structure of Competitive Industry* (1959); and Dennis H. Robertson, *Money* (1959). All three were written by eminent economists, students and followers of Marshall, and all were intended for the person who has no prior knowledge of economics. By contrast, it might be interesting to dip into the ultimate statement of fully developed neoclassical economics, Paul A. Samuelson, *Foundations of Economic Analysis* (Cambridge, Mass.: Harvard University Press, 1947), but bring your calculus along and be prepared for heavy going.

Although surveys of modern economics tend, of necessity, to be highly selective, two general works are T. W. Hutchison, *A Review of Economic Doctrines: 1870–1929* (London: Oxford University Press, 1953), which is essentially a historical summary of major trends, and Ben B. Seligman, *Main Currents in Modern Economics* (Glencoe, Ill.: The Free Press, 1962), a broad and inclusive volume full of useful insights into the social theories and political assumptions underlying the scientific doctrines of academic economics. Paul T. Homan, *Contempo-*

rary Economic Thought (New York: Harper and Brothers, 1928) is an
older but useful book that emphasizes the split between neoclassical
theorists and institutionalists led by Veblen. Abram L. Harris, *Economics
and Social Reform* (New York: Harper and Brothers, 1958), covers
somewhat the same ground with a broader perspective and the advantage of a longer view.

Allan G. Gruchy, *Modern Economic Thought* (New York: Prentice-
Hall, Inc., 1947) is a laudatory survey of Veblen and other institutional-
ists. Rexford G. Tugwell, ed., *The Trend of Economics* (New York:
Alfred A. Knopf, Inc., 1924) presents essays by the leading American
institutionalist economists that emphasize both their criticisms of orthodox economics and their advocacy of economic reforms. Two books by
J. M. Clark, *Preface to Social Economics* (New York: Farrar and Rinehart,
1936) and *The Social Control of Business* (New York: McGraw-Hill Book
Company, 1939) develop those themes further, as do the essays of
Wesley Mitchell in *The Backward Art of Spending Money* (New York:
McGraw-Hill Book Company, 1937). John R. Commons was a prolific,
obtuse, and turgid writer; his books are almost impossible to read—with
one exception, his fascinating autobiography, *Myself* (Madison: Uni-
versity of Wisconsin Press, 1964). The best of Veblen's thought is in
The Theory of the Leisure Class (New York: Mentor Books, 1954) and *The
Theory of Business Enterprise* (New York: Mentor Books); his essays in
The Place of Science in Modern Civilization (New York: Russell and
Russell, Inc., 1961) are also interesting.

The best introduction to the Fabian socialists is still George
Bernard Shaw, ed., *Fabian Essays* (London: George Allen and Unwin,
1948). Most of Hobson's works are out of print, except for *Imperialism*
(London: George Allen and Unwin, 1902), but three of Tawney's works
are available in inexpensive editions: *Religion and the Rise of Capitalism*
(New York: Mentor Books, 1947), *The Acquisitive Society* (New York:
Harcourt, Brace, & World, Inc., 1960), and *Equality* (New York:
Capricorn Books, 1961). The papal encyclicals on social problems,
Rerum Novarum, Quadragesimo Anno, and *Mater et Magistra*, are readily
available in pamphlets published by The American Press or the
Paulist Press.

Keynes' *General Theory of Employment* (New York: Harcourt, Brace
& World, Inc., 1936) is far too difficult for the ordinary reader. One
might start with *The Economic Consequences of the Peace* (New York:
Harcourt, Brace, & World, Inc., 1920), *The Means to Prosperity* (New
York: Harcourt, Brace & World, Inc., 1933), or *Essays and Sketches in
Biography* (New York: Meridian Books, 1956). Two good summary-
introductions to the *General Theory* are Dudley Dillard, *The Economics of
John Maynard Keynes* (New York: Prentice-Hall, Inc., 1948) and Alvin
Hansen, *A Guide to Keynes* (New York: McGraw-Hill Book Company,
1953). R. F. Harrod, *The Life of John Maynard Keynes* (London: Mac-

145

INDEX OF NAMES

A
Altgeld, John Peter, 70
Aristotle, 73
Arkwright, Richard, 22
Ayres, Leonard, 93

B
Baer, George F., 71
Bagehot, Walter, 78
Bakewell, Robert, 22
Barone, Enrico, 115, 116
Becon, Thomas, 1, 2
Bentham, Jeremy, 18, 32, 45-48, 72
Berle, Adolf, 93, 128, 129
Besant, Annie, 88
Boecke, J. H., 118
Böhm-Bawerk, Eugen, 81, 101
Bowley, Arthur, 103
Boyle, Robert, 19
Bryan, William Jennings, 90-91
Bukharin, Nikolai, 111, 112
Burke, Edmund, 23, 33

C
Carnegie, Andrew, 66, 67, 68, 69, 79
Catchings, Waddill, 103
Cleveland, Grover, 70
Colbert, Jean Baptiste, 10

Colm, Gerhard, 107
Commons, John R., 93, 94
Conwell, Russell, 68
Crompton, Samuel, 22

D
Darwin, Charles, 62, 79, 84
Debs, Eugene, 70
Dickens, Charles, 50
Disraeli, Benjamin, 50
Domar, Evsey, 126, 127
Douglas, Clifford, 103
Du Pont de Nemours, Pierre, 13

E
Ely, Richard T., 93
Engels, Friedrich, 54

F
Fabricant, Solomon, 130, 131
Field, Cyrus, 64
Field, David Dudley, 64
Field, Stephen J., 64, 65, 75, 79
Fisher, Irving, 82, 103, 104
Fisk, Jim, 68
Forster, E. M., 99
Foster, William T., 103
Fox, Charles James, 33
Franklin, Benjamin, 5
Fry, Roger, 99

G

Galbraith, John Kenneth, 126, 131, 136
Gesell, Silvio, 103
Ginsberg, Eli, 131
Gould, Jay, 68
Gournay, Vincent de, 12
Grotius, Hugo, 20

H

Halley, Edmund, 19
Hamilton, Walton, 93
Hammarskjöld, Dag, 102
Hansen, Alvin, 107
Hargreaves, James, 22
Harrod, R. F., 126, 127
Harvey, William, 19
Hayek, Friedrich von, 116
Hayes, Rutherford B., 64
Hobbes, Thomas, 20
Hobson, John A., 87, 88, 90
Holmes, Oliver Wendell, 66
Hood, Thomas, 50
Hoover, Herbert, 78
Hornick, Phillip von, 9
Hume, David, 14, 15, 18, 21
Huxley, Aldous, 136

J

Jefferson, Thomas, 14
Jevons, William Stanley, 73, 77
John XXIII, Pope, 87

K

Kay, John, 22
Keynes, John Maynard, 98-108, 109, 119, 121, 125, 127
Keynes, John Neville, 99
Khrushchev, Nikita, 114, 121
Kuznets, Simon, 103

L

Lange, Oscar, 116
Lavoisier, Antoine, 19
Lenin, V. I., 88, 110, 111

Leo XIII, Pope, 85, 86
Liberman, Yevsei, 114
Lincoln, Abraham, 14, 64
Locke, John, 15, 20
Lynd, Robert and Helen, 93

M

Malthus, Thomas R., 32, 34-37, 44
Mandeville, Bernard de, 14, 15
Marshall, Alfred, 74, 76, 99
Marx, Karl, 28, 53-60, 61, 71, 72, 73, 74, 75, 76, 80, 81, 84, 88, 110, 122
Means, Gardner, 93, 128, 129
Menger, Karl, 73, 74, 81
Mill, James, 43, 44, 48
Mill, John Stuart, 43-44, 48
Mills, C. Wright, 93
Mises, Ludwig von, 115, 116
Mitchell, Wesley, 93
Morgan, J. P., 69
Myrdal, Gunnar, 102, 119

N

Newton, Isaac, 19
North, Dudley, 14, 15

O

Ohlin, Bertil, 102
Orwell, George, 136
Owen, Robert, 51-53, 60

P

Paine, Thomas, 33
Parrington, Vernon, 93
Pigou, Arthur, 116
Pitt, William, 18, 33
Pius XI, Pope, 87
Prebisch, Raúl, 119, 120
Preobrazhenski, Evgeni, 111
Price, Richard, 18
Proudhon, Pierre Joseph, 53
Pullman, George, 70

Q
Quesnay, François, 13, 18

R
Ricardo, David, 32, 37-40, 41, 44, 48, 74, 75, 104
Robertson, D. H., 102
Roosevelt, Franklin D., 63, 78, 94, 97, 106
Rostow, W. W., 118, 119

S
Samuelson, Paul, 135
Say, Jean Baptiste, 32, 41-45, 77, 78
Schumpeter, Joseph, 121, 122, 123, 124
Shaw, George Bernard, 88
Sidgwick, Henry, 80
Sismondi, Jean Simonde de, 43
Slichter, Sumner H., 130
Smith, Adam, 14, 17-31, 32, 33, 41, 43, 47, 74, 79, 82
Smith, Hubert Llewellyn, 77
Soddy, Frederick, 103
Sombart, Werner, 89
Spence, William, 43
Spencer, Herbert, 62, 63, 66, 75, 79
Spinoza, Baruch, 21
Sprague, Oliver M. W., 78
Stalin, Joseph, 111, 112, 114, 117
Strachey, Lytton, 99
Sumner, William Graham, 62, 63, 75, 79

T
Tawney, Richard H., 87, 89, 90
Taylor, Fred M., 116
Theobald, Robert, 136
Thornton, Henry, 44
Tilden, Samuel J., 64
Townshend, Charles, 18, 22
Trotsky, Leon, 111, 112
Tugan-Baranowsky, Michel, 101
Tull, Jethro, 22
Turgot, Jacques, 13, 18

V
Vanderbilt, William, 68
Veblen, Thorstein, 90, 91, 92, 93

W
Wallas, Graham, 88
Walras, Léon, 74
Webb, Beatrice, 88
Webb, Sidney, 88
Weber, Max, 89
Weiser, Friedrich von, 81
Wells, H. G., 88
Whitney, Eli, 22
Wicksell, Knut, 101, 102
Wicksteed, Philip, 81
Wilson, Thomas, 1, 2
Woolf, Virginia, 99
Wright, Carroll, 77

Y
Young, Arthur, 22